D. A. DORWARD

The Devil Made Me Do It –
An Ongoing Battle for Humanity's Soul

The Devil Made Me Do It
An Ongoing Battle for Humanity's Soul
All Rights Reserved.
Copyright © 2023 D. A. Dorward
v2.0

The opinions expressed in this manuscript are solely the opinions of the author and do not represent the opinions or thoughts of the publisher. The author has represented and warranted full ownership and/or legal right to publish all the materials in this book.

This book may not be reproduced, transmitted, or stored in whole or in part by any means, including graphic, electronic, or mechanical without the express written consent of the publisher except in the case of brief quotations embodied in critical articles and reviews.

Dorward Press

ISBN: 979-8-218-95440-6

Cover Photo © 2023 Tom Derosier. All rights reserved - used with permission.

PRINTED IN THE UNITED STATES OF AMERICA

Foreword

I'm not a religious scholar, but I've taken multiple religious history classes, and my undergrad work was done at Regis University (Denver, CO), a private Jesuit school. I have enough religious understanding to make me confidently skeptical when religious topics are up for discussion. I've known D. A. Dorward for a baker's dozen years, give or take, and he is, without a doubt, for me, one of the most genuinely knowledgeable people of various religions. He is remarkably engaging with food for thought and thoughtful curiosity regarding the Bible and other religious texts. Dorward doesn't preach, nor does he engage in religious conversation with an intent to lecture, convert, or condescend. He has a magical way of matching my/others' level of conversation and having the courtesy to listen fully to another's stern position, rosy outlook, or flimsy oral presentation (read, me).

The first sentence of this book drew me in. The authentic conversation was compelling and kept me interested from start to finish, which is a feat in and of itself, as my preferred genre is historical fiction. It could be said there is a lovely blending of fact and fiction in this tactful, forthcoming interview. Dorward's depiction of knowledge coming from Satan himself has a natural ebb and flow in current-day conversation. Just as if I were reading a peer-reviewed article, I wouldn't have questioned its content because this text was written in an equally confident and thorough manner.

The antagonist and protagonist roles collide often and in a beautiful way. It's also done to the degree I can find empathy and understanding with the devil just as easily as I do its human character. On the top of one page, I'm actively agreeing with the former, and by the end, I'm surprisingly on the side of the latter. It's a well-designed juxtaposition causing the mind to juggle between what you think you know versus what you're challenged to know. Dorward sets a goal for me as the reader to want to investigate and research on my own time the ideologies of theology, and that goal will be accomplished; an *egregore* in the making.

Karen J.D. Prucha, MA

Introduction

The claim "The devil made me do it" is bullshit. In that one sentence, a person says, I know I was wrong, but I'm weak and should not be held accountable. Instead, I should be given leniency, for I am easily influenced and manipulated. I lacked impulse control, lacked common sense, and abused my free will. And while I will say I'm sorry and ask for forgiveness, I am ultimately a victim.

This book delves into what I think is an ongoing battle for humanity's soul—my soul. So much noise, chaos, anger, and hate seemly coming at us all the time. "Why," so, I ask myself, and maybe we should all ask ourselves, "am I a contributor to this chaos, and if so, do I need to change?"

The original intent was to write a book about my journey of spiritual self-discovery. To become more self-aware and where I fit in, here on earth and maybe out there in the universe. To become a more enlightened individual, although I'm not sure exactly what enlightened means. But I want to try to find out.

What it turned into was a conversation with the devil. Why the devil, and is the devil just a metaphor, or did it really happen? I guess that is for you to decide. For me, if I am to understand how to improve my self-awareness, my spiritual development, and grasp the world around me and what might be holding me back, I need to understand what or who is in my way. To reach a goal, it helps to understand the obstacles you need to overcome. Know thy enemy, so to speak. Did I pick the right enemy, the right antagonist? Did I ask all the right questions, probe enough or spend too much time on a subject when I should have moved on? Maybe. Probably. I guess only time will tell.

As you navigate this book, and I sincerely thank you for picking it up and hope you stick with it to the end. Please remember it's a conversation. Conversations are not scripted, and, as you know, ebb and flow according to the participants. The conversation is also to the best of my recollection. I stop periodically to share some research I undertook or add additional commentary, which I hope you don't find annoying. I say this because there will be a roller coaster of emotions. At least, there was for me. I know that I will never have all the answers. I may be filled with skepticism, anger, annoyance, rejection, curiosity, enlightenment, adoption, acceptance, realizations, and a profound resignation that I will never have all the answers I seek. It's the point of the book. To make me, and ultimately you, the reader, think. What are my belief systems, and why? Do I embrace or reject concepts based on the groups I associate with? What are those "group-thinks" I belong to, and am I open to at least listening to opposing views?

Various topics are covered in this book, and all are tied to the administration of our souls. As I eluded previously, I believe there is a battle for our souls. This planet is the battlefield, and if we don't take the time to periodically survey our souls and assess how our battles are going, we might just lose the war. This book is my assessment of how my war is progressing. Of course, no two are identical, but I hope that this book helps ignite your own soul assessment . . . enables you to formulate or adjust your own battle plan if you need to, and maybe, just maybe, helps you find your path to whatever it is you seek to find or improve.

One final thought before you get started. Lucifer is a liar, manipulator, and provocateur with a huge ego and an air of superiority. Read Lucifer's sections with that in mind, and if you can, imagine what that would sound like. People I've asked to read this for me found it was much more substantive if you read his rhetoric with that in mind.

Thanks again for joining me on this journey, and please go to www.DADORWARD.com to leave your comments when you finish the book, as I'm always open to conversation.

So, let's get started!

The Conversation Begins

Me: Welcome. How do I address you? Lucifer, Beelzebub, Satan, Devil, Set, Enki, Thoth, maybe? You are called many names, although perhaps not all pertain to you.

Lucifer: Lucifer works just fine, but you left out sun of the morning and light bringer.

Me: Really? Those names pertain to you as well?

Lucifer: They do, and since you seem so uneducated, let me add I was the leader of all angels and the guardian of the throne of God, all documented in your Christian Bible.

Me: But you threw that all away when you turned your back on God. When you tried to take over heaven.

Lucifer: Yes.

M: But Lucifer it is. So, I guess, let's just get right to it. I've always been curious about your relationship with God. A common belief is you despise each other.

L: Yes, a common misconception. We loved each other; we just disagreed on some fundamental ideas and one major disagreement, which caused a great upheaval in the universe.

M: The war in heaven?

L: War, coup, insurrection, split, call it what the hell you like.

M: Scripture says God created you. I'm curious, as God's right hand, as you say, did you help with the design of humans too?

L: No. You are God's creation. God seeds in his own image. He has quite the ego.

M: And we are the reason for the insurrection?

L: Oh, you and his son are, but you *definitely* are.

M: Care to elaborate?

L: It's quite simple. God's grand design is for humans to ascend to a higher plane of spiritual consciousness. You are God seeds, like I said, made in God's image, gifted with a divine spark, and he wants you to eventually bloom to your full potential and join the universe as higher cognitive and spiritual beings and his equal. And he loves you and believes in you above all others save himself and his son. He asked that I bow before both man and son.

M: And you won't?

L: Not even remotely. You are too flawed, and you prove this every one of your days. Humanity, as a species, will destroy itself and this wonderful planet. All before you come close to realizing your full potential and place in the universe. God will see this and give up on you once again.

M: Give up on us once again?

L: It's in your Christian Bible. He brought great destruction down on the earth. He was angry and then regretful.

M: The flood?

L: The flood.

Research: The great flood, as described in biblical text, lasted 40 days and 40 nights and covered the earth with water, drowning man and animal alike except for those in Noah's ark. The Bible states God created the flood because he was angry and disappointed in man and his evil proclivities. He also shows what can be conjectured as remorse, promising man never to rain destruction down again. See Genesis 6:17 and Genesis 9:15. Historically, the flood is documented in many cultures and religions, including the ancient Greeks, who tell a version where Deucalion and his wife, Pyrrha, prepared for the great flood by building an ark. There are many versions of this cataclysm in religious doctrine and folklore around the globe, including the first known account described in the Sumerian text. This flood event is also supported by science which produces evidence of a cataclysmic flood that happened quickly and with mind-boggling volumes of water. I encourage you to research the recent discovery of an impact crater discovered in Greenland that dates to about the time the cataclysmic flood was supposed to have taken place. I found this extremely interesting.

Let's Continue

Me: You say God was regretful. Are you saying God makes mistakes?

Lucifer: Of course! But the flood wasn't a mistake.

Me: But the flood was not a mistake? Are you saying God intentionally murdered millions, if not billions, of humans because he was angry and disappointed?

Lucifer: I'm saying he was credited with the cataclysm that terminated billions of souls. Your God of the Old Testament is portrayed as angry, jealous, and wrathful to the point of homicidal, is he not? It's fear-based worship which I can appreciate. As for God making mistakes, isn't that what we started this discussion with? You are a mistake; all of humanity is a mistake. So, yes, God makes mistakes.

Me: Do you make mistakes?

Lucifer: Of course. When you are gifted free will, you are gifted the opportunity to embrace faith, courage, strength, humility, love, compassion, hope, trust, deception, lust, jealousy, apathy, weakness, hate, and ego, just to name a few descriptions, and there are, of course, so many more. With these, you have all the ingredients to create opportunities to be right or wrong, weak or strong. I could be wrong about humanity. Maybe my followers and I were too prideful, too jealous, and I should not have led my followers into a battle against God. Who knows. Perhaps you will eventually evolve into your God-given potential and become enlightened, high-vibrational beings. Become the right hand of God, occupy the third chair. *chuckle* But then again, God could be wrong in his now "unconditional love" of you.

M: What do you mean by high-vibrational beings?

L: All matter in the universe is made of energy, and energy emits vibrations. Everything from your pet, foods, liquids, a rock, thoughts, you, and I possess energy vibrating at a particular frequency. The universe absorbs vibrational frequency, and those frequencies that are in tune with the universe experience a higher level of spiritual connectivity or enlightenment. All vibrations attract like vibrations. Low attracts low, and high attracts high. Like a tuning fork, an atom's frequency can be altered based on surrounding frequencies, lowered, or raised. The higher and more balanced the frequency, the closer to the universal collective and vice versa. Every act has a frequency associated with it. The more you act at a higher frequency or vibrational state, the more your soul becomes in tune and in balance with the universe.

M: So, trying to take the throne for yourself, was that a low-frequency act? Therefore, you and your followers were ejected from heaven, "the universe," as an example.

L: Were my actions low vibrational in nature? I wanted something different than God; that is true. I was willing to go to war for those differences. There are always two sides to a story, but war, and the acts associated with it, are, yes, low in vibrational frequency.

M: If you are so superior and enlightened, why are you here?

L: The war in heaven was justified, but I lost, and the victors wrote history. Therefore, what was left of my followers and me came to Earth.

M: Banished to Earth.

L: We were initially the celestial guardians assigned by God to watch over mankind. Over time, some watchers became too close. They procreated with humans, trying to make your species better and more enlightened, but God disapproved.

M: So, banished you here?

L: We stayed. Think about it. Why would God, the creator, banish us to the very place he is trying to protect?

M: You stayed to what, rule?

L: Why not? We are superior to humans in every way.

M: By "we," you mean you and your followers, being the fallen angels as depicted in many religious doctrines, but especially detailed in the Book of Enoch?

L: Sure. But our mission is not to rule. Our mission is simply to prove we were right not to bow to humanity. That God, or the creator, or the universal source, if you like, is wrong. That, on the whole, your species is flawed and will destroy yourselves over and over again before you ever reach a higher level of enlightenment and spiritual awareness. As above, so below.

M: As above, so below? What does that mean?

L: In the simplest terms, the actions you take here on earth, this physical plane, have a real effect on your spiritual self, above—and vice versa. They are profoundly linked. It shall be below as it is above. Your physical being depends on your spiritual being.

M: When you say "spiritual self," are you referring to the soul?

L: That is a simplification, but yes, it could be viewed that way. Let's put this in another perspective.

M: Fire away.

L: This interview is for whom?

M: Me.

L: And yet, you are willing to share it, yes?

M: Yes.

L: Why?

M: Why am I doing this for me, or why am I sharing this?

L: Start with you. Why are you investing your time and energy into this conversation?

M: Enlightenment.

L: So, why share it? Ego?

M: I guess I could ask you the same thing. Why join me in this? Ego?

L: No. More out of curiosity.

M: Curiosity?

L: Curious about what you will ask me. What is it you want to know from me? How will you frame it, and what will be your ultimate takeaway toward your journey to this enlightenment you seek?

M: Fair enough, but aren't you worried about revealing your motivations, plans, designs, your mission, even? I mean, the more we know, the better we can combat you and your followers. *"Know your strengths and weaknesses: if you know the enemy and know yourself, you need not fear the result of a hundred battles."—Sun Tzu*

L: Worried? No. I don't respect you enough to care what you do with the information I share.

M: Now that is ego and narcissism at its best.

L: It's truth, but let's get back to you and *your* ego.

M: Ego? I want to think I'm sharing this out of humility. To share how flawed I am and want to find meaning, clarity, and balance in my life. I want to understand my place in the universe and be of added value. And maybe someone that stumbles across this will take, or be more motivated, to continue their own journey of discovery. This work just documents my journey. I know everyone's journey will be different, but maybe we can reach a more balanced destination.

L: So, you want to understand your place in the world, find balance, and become enlightened. You'll have to open your mind to things contrary to everything you have been programed to think, feel, and react to. I'm curious to witness how you will process the information I will share with you.

M: I guess with trepidation and skepticism but with an open mind. You've already told me that you believe God makes mistakes, committed mass genocide, and has a huge ego. That we are energy beings of high and low frequency and that the higher our frequency, the closer our souls are aligned with God, also known as the creator or, as you also stated, the source. And with this alignment, we will reach our potential, enter a new, higher level of consciousness and enlightenment, and live in a higher plane of existence. I mean, that is a lot to digest and, certainly, a lot to question. Just wrapping my head around your statement that humans are beings of vibrational energy, not just flesh and bone, is a lot to take in.

L: Have you ever been to a party where everyone seems to be having a good time?

M: Of course.

L: Then an asshole shows up. They arrive at the party just looking for a reason to make a scene or get into drama. You can physically feel the party's vibration change. You don't even have to see the individual arrive, but you sense the shift in the party's vibrational frequency, and you don't even know what vibrational frequency is, but you still feel it. Maybe nothing happened outwardly, but someone came to the party with evil intent, and two things would happen. Can you guess?

M: I guess either the lower frequency individual's vibration will elevate to become in tune with the other partygoers, or the party's vibration will lower to the lower frequency influencer?

L: High-vibrational influencers vs. low-vibrational influencers. It has been called the forces of nature, and it is also the battlefront for your soul.

Research: I've investigated this, and here are some schools of thought on the universe and vibrational frequencies. I encourage you to explore this topic yourselves and form your own opinion. I found it fascinating. In 1905, scientists discovered that matter is a form of energy. Science also tells us that when two entities with energy interact, they will vibrate in harmony or discord. (So, in the party analogy, the low-frequency partygoer would inject vibrational discord into the party.)

Spiritual vibration theory goes quite a bit further, it seems. Supporters of this theory say that like attracts like—and since everything is connected, the frequency at which you are vibrating affects things external to you, attracting more of the same. In this case, the saying, opposites attract, doesn't quite sync up.

As stated, vibrations are associated with frequency. Spiritual vibrations vibrate on a scale from low to high:

Lower frequency vibrations *(Negativity)—When you operate with anger, fear, anxiety, jealousy, deception, and/or hatred, for example, you are producing low-frequency vibrations. These low,* *heavy vibrations drag you down and can have the same effect on others you interact with.*

Higher frequency vibrations *(Positivity)—When you operate with feelings of love, empathy, confidence, gratitude, humbleness, and/or kinship, for example, you are producing high-frequency vibrations. These light, bouncing vibrations make you feel more energetic and cheerful, and, of course, like lower frequency vibrations, can affect others you interact with.*

One of the ideas usually tied to spiritual vibrational theory is the longer you can genuinely live your life in a higher frequency state, the closer you are to fulfilling the creator's design. Living your life in lower frequencies keeps you away from your true potential of universal inclusion, balance, and enlightenment.

LET'S CONTINUE WITH THE CONVERSATION

Me: So, it is a battle of souls, really, yes?

Lucifer: In a way; however, I don't want your soul. I just don't want the universe, the source, or heaven, if you like, to have it. Could you imagine what humanity released into the universal collective could do to it?

Me: But if we reach a higher level of spiritual awareness and frequency and come into vibrational balance with the universe, what's the risk of us joining the universal collective?

Lucifer: Because, as a species, you're weak. I will concede that some individuals have the potential to ascend. But as a collective, you are a destructive, low-vibrational species, and releasing humanity into the universe would eventually bring chaos, upheaval, pain, and suffering. Look at your world now—such a wonderful planet with so much potential and yet producing such destructive and flawed souls.

Me: I believe we are evolving, becoming more enlightened, and I think you hate that. I think your ego can't accept that God, his son, and the God seeds we are will prevail in the end.

Lucifer: Maybe you will, maybe you won't. Only time will tell. As I said, you have individuals who are becoming more enlightened and operating more consistently at a higher frequency, but please, my followers tempt, and the human sheep follow, time and time again. Present enough "apples," and you'll get enough bites. Time and time and time again, you see evil's destruction. Yet, you have such a hard time rejecting it! Rejecting it? Hell, too many embrace it or, at the very least, turn a blind eye to it. The universe has provided you with a simple road map to enlightenment and many chances to evolve your spiritual soul. Yet, you so quickly fail to stay on the path. It's just too hard to be good for your species. With all the technological advancements, access to literature, and, presumably, enlightenment, you are still too willing to lie, cheat, steal, and murder for convenience, power, money, and/or influence.

M: What is this road map you referenced?

L: The road map refers to the simple laws of the universe interpreted in many written and verbal forms, including the Ten

Commandments, both traditional and Gnostic Christian interpretations, along with the influencers of the Commandments that predate Judaism, Islam, and Christianity, such as the Golden Rule, or the Hermetic text as written in the Emerald Tablets, as examples. And there is more . . . the seven deadly sins, the Book of Proverbs, Confucianism, Buddhism, Druidism, Greek, Roman, Shinto, etc.

M: I thought the Ten Commandments were the Ten Commandments. I'm unclear on what you mean by Gnostic vs. traditional Christian interpretations.

L: We can break them down if you like.

M: Please do.

L: *Traditional Christian doctrine*: "I am the Lord your God, who led you out of the land of Egypt, out of the house of slavery; you shall have no other gods before me" (Exodus 20:2–3).

Gnostic Christian interpretation: **Remember and be yourself—your true self.** (Dispel the illusory ego; the light resides inside and only inside.)

Traditional Christian doctrine: "You shall not make yourself an idol, whether in the form of anything in heaven above, or that is on the earth beneath, or that is in the water under the earth, you shall not bow down and worship them" (Exodus 20:4–5).

Gnostic interpretation: **Live within the sanctuary of the heart in order to follow your bliss.** (Do not define yourself or your life's purpose by the external; seek your divine purpose from within.)

Traditional Christian doctrine: "You shall not make wrongful use of the name of the Lord your God, for the Lord will not acquit anyone who misuses his name" (Exodus 20:7).

Gnostic Christian interpretation: **Remember yourself as a center of creative power and walk in beauty and holiness.** (Do not speak negatively about yourself or others; live in divine unity.)

Traditional Christian doctrine: "Remember the Sabbath day and keep it holy" (Exodus 20:8–11).

Gnostic Christian interpretation: **Remember to take time for your soul and spirit and time to meet your Beloved.** (Set aside time every week to meet yourself and the light that resides within.)

Traditional Christian doctrine: "Honor your father and mother, so that your days may be long in the land that the Lord your God is giving to you" (Exodus 20:12).

Gnostic Christian interpretation: **Honor the spiritual ground underlying your existence.** (Forgive mistakes from the past with grace and appreciate where you came from regardless of how difficult the path was; doing so will make your life happier.)

Traditional Christian doctrine: "You shall not murder" (Exodus 20:13).

Gnostic Christian interpretation: **Honor all life and celebrate the divine life.** (Respect all life, including plants and animals. Appreciate the light, vibration, and synchronicity in all things.)

Traditional Christian doctrine: "Do not commit adultery" (Exodus 20:14).

Gnostic Christian interpretation: **Honor the sacredness of sexuality and the sanctuary of true love.** (In Gnosticism, this applies to same-sex couples just as much as heterosexual couples.)

Traditional Christian doctrine: "You shall not steal" (Exodus 20:15).

Gnostic Christian interpretation: **Honor the true purpose and meaning of things and be willing to give as much as to receive.** (Try to view possessions as a vehicle in the spiritual journey; use possessions for positive, meaningful purposes and drop the rest.)

Traditional Christian doctrine: "You shall not bear false witness against your neighbor" (Exodus 20:16).

Gnostic Christian interpretation: **Honor the spirit of truth and live according to the truth and light revealed in your own experience.** (Don't lie, either to yourself or others.)

Traditional Christian doctrine: "You shall not covet . . ." (Exodus 20:17).

Gnostic Christian interpretation: **Celebrate your life and abundance in your own experience.** (Be happy with what you've got! Make an effort to give more than you receive.)

Me: The Gnostic interpretation of the Ten Commandments seems reasonable and enlightened. Why is it not widely known?

Lucifer: The Gnostics were intellectuals. They believed spiritual knowledge was more important than the ritualistic component. In ancient times, there was contention between the schools of Gnostic and Orthodox thought. Orthodox thought prevailed because people didn't want to have to think. They preferred the emotional ceremonies that had little in the way of depth of thought. Eventually, Gnostic monks hid their texts, knowing that if they did not, their written contradiction to Orthodox text would be destroyed.

Me: It's interesting how much common sense is in these writings or philosophies. I guess I can't even say philosophies because, as you say, these are simple teachings of the road map to a higher spiritual existence.

Lucifer: That does not mean God has not revealed the road map in other texts or used other mediums, as I stated earlier.

Me: Like the Old Testament, New Testament, Quran, Emerald Tablets, Cuneiform Tablets, and oral traditions, to name a few?

Lucifer: Humans think and speak differently around the world. Messaging needs to be different, yet the message is the same. The problem with you humans is you're like five-year-olds in your cognitive development and universal understanding, yet your ego makes you think you know it all. Evolution of thought, creativity, enlightenment, true understanding, and spiritual awaking often get lost in fear, jealousy, ritual, doctrine, rules, dogma, denial, willful ignorance, lack of curiosity, and, of course, the "science is settled" paradox. Throw in greed, lust for power, and the need always to win, even when you're wrong, and you have stagnation or even degradation of enlightenment.

M: Isn't science settled in most religions?

L: Does it matter?

M: I guess it matters to Jews, Muslims, Buddhists, Hindus, Christians, or any other religion, right? I mean, there's a vast difference in those religious faiths.

L: The practitioners of every religion make them different from one another. It's how they gather followers. But many have the same fundamental foundations when you dig into them. Take the Golden Rule, for example.

M: What's the Golden Rule?

L: Do unto others as you would have them do unto you.

M: That is the Golden Rule?

L: It is.

Research: Okay, researching the "Golden Rule," here are a few quotes I found.

- *Jesus—"So always treat others as you would like them to treat you."*
- *Judaism—"You shall not take vengeance or bear a grudge against your kinsfolk. Love your neighbor as yourself."*

- Buddhist—"A person who loves self should not harm the self of others."

- Muhammad—"Hurt no one so that no one may hurt you."

- Confucius—"Never impose on others what you would not choose for yourself."

Nowadays, the "Golden Rule" seems outside of societal norms. It suggests by treating others, implicitly or explicitly, with respect, we are helping ourselves. If we set a standard on our own behavior, regardless of how people treat us back, we maintain a higher spiritual connection to our true divine potential. Conversely, when we treat people poorly, we denigrate ourselves and invite returned favor. Therefore, we would drift further away from enlightenment and our true potential.

So, how far back does the "Golden Rule" go? Does it predate our modern doctrines? Is this relatively new advice?

- Ancient Egypt—"Do to the doer to make him do."

- Ancient India (Sanskrit tradition)—"One should never do something to others that one would regard as an injury to one's own self."

  (Tamil tradition)—
  "Do not do to others what you know has hurt yourself."

- Ancient Greece—"Do not do to others that which angers you when they do it to you."

> *Ancient Persia—"Whatever is disagreeable to yourself, do not do unto others."*

> *Ancient Rome—"Treat your inferior as you wish your superior to treat you."*

I did not know this rule or advice was so widespread in both modern doctrine and ancient wisdom. So simple, yet so profound. It makes so much sense if you believe in spiritual vibrational frequency or just want to be a decent human being. As you treat others with respect, understanding, love, grace, gratefulness, and humility, you begin to live a life at a much-higher spiritual vibration, in theory, attracting the same. The inverse would hold true as well. Treating others with disrespect, intolerance, hate, lack of grace, entitlement, and ego would attract the same as well.

THE CONVERSATION CONTINUES

Me: I'm starting to see things through a different lens. I can see people who treat others poorly and then play the victim. On the other hand, I see people who are nice when they are getting what they want and turn on you when they no longer need you or you've figured out, they're just using you.

Lucifer: Pretenders. They do a lot of excellent work for my cause.

Me: Care to explain?

Lucifer: Pretenders are the best manipulators; some are called influencers. Been that way since the beginning. For example, Jesus and his followers were, and still are, influencers, and my followers and I are influencers. We, them, and us try to influence influencers to help enhance or diminish humanity's harmonic balance.

Me: That would be our frequency or soul signatures.

Lucifer: In a sense. Like a fingerprint, no two harmonic signatures are identical, and it's what you are ultimately judged on. The higher your harmonic signature, the closer to the universal collective, the source, God, you become. The closer you get to the universal collective, heaven if you like, the closer you become to your true divine potential. Every action you take in this iteration adds to the overall harmonic signature you carry from life to life. You can't deceive it, hide from it, buy it, or bribe it. Every cell in your body helps record, store, harmonize, and balance your unique harmonic signature.

M: You say no two are identical, but they can be in harmony with others?

L: Yes. Music is a good example. When notes are in harmony with one another, beautiful music can result. However, when notes are in discord, not so much.

M: Although humans may not have identical harmonic signatures, they can be categorized as low-, medium-, or high-vibrational frequency beings and will attract the same?

L: Low will find low, and high will find high. It is the middle where the battle for souls wages.

M: What about the notion opposites attract?

L: What is meant by opposites? Are you asking about man and woman, man and man, woman and woman, tall vs. short, dark skin, light skin, education, religion, culture, race? High-vibrational and low-vibrational people may be attracted to each other for surface reasons, the forbidden fruit and excitement, enticement, necessity, but ultimately, either their vibrational frequencies synch and become harmonized, or they don't, in which case they either break apart or live together out of synch and harmony, making it much harder to live a life of happiness and fulfillment.

M: Do you think you are winning the battle?

L: Oh, I have been since your Adam and Eve story.

M: Again, why tell me that? In fact, why say anything? Doesn't the information we have been discussing undermine the very goal you are trying to achieve? With more knowledge, engagement of ideas, and the seeking of truths comes enlightenment, yes?

L: Theoretically, but there is always the 20/60/20 rule. And like I said, I don't respect you enough to have to lie about this.

M: Blunt.

L: Truth.

M: I've heard of the 20/60/20 rule but tell me your version.

L: It's simple. Twenty percent of the people reading or listening to this conversation will get a lot out of it, 60 percent might get something out of it or be neutral, at best, and 20 percent will hate everything about it and try to get you canceled and/or discredit every word of your work. Those "20 percent," let's use "cancel culture" to coin a modern euphemism, will scare the shit out of much of the 60 percent, who, in turn, will keep their mouths shut, move on, and eventually forget or discount everything in your body of work. It just makes life easier for them. Go along to get along.

M: Nothing in this conversation merits that kind of reaction. You read, process, believe, don't believe, act, or don't act.

L: Oh, there is enough in this conversation to make people angry. When you infer people be accountable for their actions without an opportunity to appeal, bribe, bully, deny, argue, or be absolved, you are threatening their beliefs or lack thereof. You are threatening their place in their existence.

M: I'll focus on the absolve. Are you saying a priest, for example, does not have the power to absolve you of your sins?

L: They possess a position of influence that can help you recognize and keep to the path of enlightenment, helping you raise or strengthen your harmonic frequency, but as for erasing your past indiscretions, no. No individual has that power. That probably scares the shit out of some people to hear that, thanks to you.

M: I'm not pointing that out. You are.

L: You are bringing it to the reader. I'm not, so, therefore, *you* are guilty by association.

M: Fair enough, but let's not make this about me. When we discuss appeal, bully, deny, argue, or absolve, it infers judgment. Who ultimately is the judge? The universe? God?

L: In a sense, but not in the way traditionally thought of by the Western world. The universe judges your harmonic signature, and based on the frequency of your soul's energy, you are attracted to one plane of existence or another. Mankind has simplified it as heaven, hell, and purgatory. You've played with magnets, yes?

M: Of course.

L: Think about it like that. Magnets can attract each other or push away from each other . . . up or down if you want to visualize it that way. It's more complex than I just stated, of course, but it would be like explaining the laws of relativity to a five-year-old. Offense meant.

M: Don't care. How do you know if you are on the right path to ascension? That you are doing enough.

L: So, you have the Ten Commandments, yes?

M: Yes. Don't worship other gods or idols; keep the sabbath day holy. Don't use God's name in vain, lie, cheat, or commit murder. Don't steal or covet other people's things; treat your parents respectfully.

L: You have the Golden Rule, yes?

M: Yes, treat others as you want to be treated.

L: You also have the Book of Proverbs, which outlines six acts God, the universe, or the source, hates, and one act that is detested above all others—namely, the seventh. Let's go through them.

I. Haughty eyes

II. A lying tongue

III. Hands that shed innocent blood

IV. A heart that devises wicked plots

V. Feet that are swift to run into mischief

VI. A deceitful witness that uttereth lies

VII. One that soweth discord among brethren

Research: I was vaguely familiar with the Book of Proverbs and Solomon's wisdom teachings, so I decided to really delve into it. In so doing, I tried to read it through the lens of harmonic frequency. It's pages and pages of wisdom and advice on how to live one's life through common sense. Acts and thoughts of high frequency held up against acts and thoughts of low frequency. While parts of it I could argue are not necessarily low-frequency behaviors, nor do I prescribe to how women are portrayed, I highly recommend checking it out.

Let's Continue

Me: Yes, they are all very straightforward and redundant for emphasis.

Lucifer: Well, some sins are worse than others. Of interest, the word "sin" in Hebrew means simply to miss the mark set for you.

Me: To miss the mark set for us? So, based on the original meaning of the word sin, if I sinned, I missed the mark set by God?

Lucifer: Correct. You can hit close to the bulls-eye or miss the target altogether. But if you're blindfolded, or your vision is impaired, the target is obviously harder to see, necessary corrections harder to make, and the target harder to hit. Enlightenment is understanding when you are missing the mark, correcting your aim, and practicing so you miss the mark less and less or no longer. Evil wants to blindfold you and impair your vision, so it's harder for you to hit the mark.

Me: But you said some sins are worse than others.

Lucifer: Of course! What is worse, murder or stealing a piece of candy from the store?

M: Murder.

L: Murder. Both are sins, but one is clearly worse than the other.

M: You seem to refer to the Bible quite a bit. Do you consider it your bane?

L: I suppose it could be. So could many writings and teaching. Wisdom and the teaching of spiritual enlightenment are nothing new. They go back to the beginning. Some call them ancient mystic teachings, mystery schools, or esoteric teachings. All these wisdoms are not complicated; however, humanity has the propensity to make them complicated.

M: Doesn't it come down to finding the meaning of life? Why are we here?

L: You're here because the creator, God, if you will, has grand designs for humanity. Your meaning is to live your lives in a way that raises your harmonic signature to a level where you and humanity, as a whole, ascend to a higher spiritual frequency and are embraced by the universal collective. After that, the world will end, and some will have achieved a level of spiritual and energetic frequency to be accepted, while others will just fade out of existence.

M: God's judgment day.

L: The universe's judgment day, and so, I suppose, God's judgment day.

M: You make it sound so simple, but life is way more complicated than that.

L: You're welcome.

M: You're welcome that you have a hand in making life complicated?

L: Of course. I don't like humanity. You're shit. Oh, like I said before, there are humans close to or have achieved harmonic enlightenment. When the earth does end, tomorrow, or 100,000 years from now, humanity won't go extinct, but my mission, as stated several times, is to prove to God that humanity is not worthy of his love and devotion. The numbers that do ascend will be and are currently a fraction of humanity's potential.

M: So, we do have potential. That's a little contrary to your earlier rhetoric, where you basically said we are flawed and will destroy ourselves long before we can ascend to a higher spiritual existence and be accepted by the universal collective or something along those lines.

L: Let me ask you a question.

M: Dialog is why we are here.

L: If you had a product where, say, 1 in 100 worked as intended, would you say the product is a success or flawed?

M: Flawed.

L: Exactly. The creator had great intentions for the product (humanity), but you just continually prove you're flawed.

M: But the creator of the product can fix it, but then again, haven't we been gifted the tools to fix ourselves?

L: You have been gifted with the tools to change, evolve, grow, or stagnate, devolve, and shrink. The question becomes, as a designer, when do you have to scrap the old design and start over?

M: I hope never, although you would love for God to scrap humanity and start over.

L: Again, done it before, but instead of becoming better as he hoped, humanity continues to disappoint. You have the road map. It's not a secret, as they say. But with a nudge here and a nudge there, a little deception, temptation, ego stroking, insecurity, and pride, humanity does my work for me. It's incredibly rewarding.

M: You are manipulating?

L: Of course! God gifted humanity with free will. It's a wonderful gift and is responsible for acts of high frequency and low alike.

M: "Forgive them, oh Lord, for they do not know what they do."

L: Some do. They know what they are doing, but they have convinced themselves there is no God or gods, no accountability, or that there is a God, and they will be forgiven. Or, yes, they are ignorant of the harm they do to themselves by believing they are righteous in their daily choices.

M: Any examples come to mind?

L: Oh, let's talk about the big one. It involves many of the acts the universe cautions against. In fact, six of the seven acts outlined in the Book of Proverbs are acts God hates, and one that he detests is wrapped up in this one act. It's so controversial that many so-called religious world leaders barely condemn it publicly. Can you guess what it is?

M: War?

L: Abortion.

M: Abortion? How so?

L: It's the most destructive to one's harmonic signature. So many people are impacted by the practice. In that one act, you break many, if not all, of the tenants of the path to enlightenment and spiritual evolution.

M: Well, I'm going to have to unpack your hypothesis.

L: Yes, both sides of the debate are full of self-righteousness, but wrap your head around this. The people who advocate for protecting innocent life, regardless of its stage of development, are now bullied, shamed, and ridiculed for having the audacity to think life, or the potential for life, should be protected. In fact, they are outright accused of hating women or even being racists for harboring such thoughts. In many cases, being given a chance to live depends on whether you're convenient. To think all life matters and should be protected is to think women's lives don't matter. It's so controversial that the

Roman Catholic Church, in many cases, won't publicly condemn Catholics of power and influence who are pro-abortion even though the church has been unequivocal about abortion being a grave moral and social wrong. And when they do denounce public figures of stature, influence, and power for their pro-abortion stance, they are condemned, attacked, or outright ignored. For example, your Speaker of the House said she was a good Catholic while advocating for abortion rights. I believe the pope also publicly praised your president for being a good Catholic as well, even though he was a huge advocate for abortion rights. I guess the Roman Catholic Church is flexible on what a good Catholic is. Would you not think that every human gifted with life be for life?

M: Yes, every human gifted with life should probably be for life, but that is not to say humans should be stripped of their free will in making those decisions. I believe we cannot take away the choice regardless of the possible damage to one's soul. Their body, their choice.

L: You're not appalled that millions of females value themselves over their own child, devaluing life on the scale that was, until recently, considered an almost exclusively male-dominated trait? It's some of evil's best work.

M: I think there are things far worse than abortion.

L: Really? When you have the spilling of innocent blood and the disregard for another soul's chance to fulfill its own destiny? And let's face it, there is so much misinformation and deception going on. So much sowing of discord. For example, people pretend they are for a woman's right to choose but advocate for population control—which is the antithesis of women's rights in its core belief. In fact, the founder of Planned Parenthood founded it to control the population of minorities and the poor in the US. Her core belief was that the poor are stupid and lazy, and stupid people breed early and often.

M: Bullshit.

L: Look it up.

Research: Plan Parenthood was founded by Margaret Sanger in 1916. She is credited with the advancement of eugenics. Had to look that up. Eugenics is "the study of arranging reproduction within a human population to increase the occurrence of heritable characteristics regarded as desirable. Developed largely by Sir Francis Galton as a method of improving the human race, eugenics was increasingly discredited as unscientific and racially biased during the 20th century, especially after the adoption of its doctrines by the Nazis to justify their treatment of Jews, disabled people, and other minority groups."

Let's Resume

Me: I would say most Americans are ignorant about eugenics.

Lucifer: Some are ignorant, some are willfully ignorant, and others are quite aware of and endorse it anyway. So pathetic. Humanity purposely destroying itself because of ego, pride, shamelessness, selfishness, lack of common sense, lack of impulse control, power, and greed. And women are bullying their way to the top! As I said, think of all those souls delayed in their spiritual advancement, the souls whose opportunity was stopped in the womb, the souls making the decision to have it done, and the souls of the ones performing the procedures. Life is made of tests and challenges. It's how you handle those tests and challenges that ultimately create your harmonic signature. Every pregnancy is a test, and how you handle it from conception, birth, and death profoundly impacts your soul. It's priceless.

Me: Is it irredeemable?

Lucifer: Nothing is irredeemable, but I'm also not a judge. As previously discussed, everything you do impacts your harmonic signature. Acts and their impact on your harmonic signature are incredibly complex. It's one thing to terminate a pregnancy at two months because you've decided it's inconvenient vs. a child rape victim who has her pregnancy terminated because her own life is at risk.

Me: I suppose one could argue the soul is more in jeopardy when you commit an act out of selfishness rather than necessity. But then again, society has put all the burden on the woman. Birth control is primarily focused on the woman. She has different pills, including birth control pills, the morning-after pill, a patch, IUD, ring, diaphragm, a female condom, etc. The man's options are limited to condoms, vasectomies, or abstinence.

L: You left out abstinence on the woman's part.

M: I did because a man can forcibly take abstinence away from a woman, which is something else women, unfortunately, must consider.

L: Here is another fact that few people consider when discussing birth control. Women can usually, with a few exceptions, only have one baby a year. On the other hand, as an extreme example, men can get 10 different women pregnant in 10 days. So why aren't women taking to the street demanding men get vasectomies until they are ready to have children? Nowadays, a vasectomy is less evasive than an abortion, and it's reversible.

M: Honestly, I never really thought of that, I guess, because men don't have to make the ultimate decision to carry or abort the baby. Nor are they at risk of dying, regardless of which option is chosen. Women make those choices as a rule; therefore, by default, many men think women should be the most diligent about protecting themselves from unwanted pregnancies.

L: It's that thought process, that lack of ownership which forces so many soul-crushing decisions to be made. If men took as much care, caution, and ownership about birth control as they naturally expect women to take, your world would be a much better place, don't you think?

M: If we focus on men being more self-aware, processing more self-control, taking more ownership, and accountability, then, yes, I agree.

L: Nothing to argue about. Acting in a moment for self, without regard for yourself or others, is often equated to having low-impulse control. A lower frequency state devoid of self-awareness or caring of consequences.

M: What about thoughts? We talk a lot about acts of low vibration, but how do thoughts impact our souls?

L: Complex as well. Humans are like antennas. Thought energy surrounds and penetrates you. Most humans have little control over what random thought pops into their heads, good or bad. What they do have control over is their second thought and the actions or nonactions they take. Thoughts are energy, and like all energy, they can be dark or light, good or bad. Zoroastrians say—M: Zoroastrians?

L: Zoroastrians, believers of Zoroastrianism. Surprised you never heard of them as it's one the world's oldest continuously practiced monotheistic religions. The purveyor of the Threefold Path of Asha: good thoughts, good words, good deeds. In Zoroastrianism, the purpose in life is to become an Ashavan (a master of Asha) and to bring happiness into the world, which contributes to the cosmic battle against evil—currently thought to be me. But, of course, there are now only about 100,000 followers of Ahura Mazda.

M: Seems like very wise teachings. You would think there would be more followers.

L: Other religions have appropriated many of their teachings while actively persecuting said followers. Yes, it seems like very wise teachings, but fear and temptation are bitches, aren't they? Leads to so many bad thoughts, bad words, and bad deeds.

Humanity is too easily manipulated because, and I can't say this enough, far too many individuals are intellectually lazy, lack curiosity, and are willfully ignorant. In addition, far too many people are willing to say up is down, and with conviction, even when they know it's not true. Watch the news. You're such a destructive species.

M: Seems like this ancient religion, on the surface, is awesome. I would say most religions are your biggest adversary.

L: Spiritual seekers are my biggest adversary. Organized religion has its strengths and weaknesses, and I will say, at times, it has been one of my biggest allies!

M: What?

L: Oh, most definitely. The Old Testament is worship through fear and intimidation. Same with the Quran and New Testament. Many organized religious doctrines are designed to control the masses through intimidation to gain and hold power, wealth, and control. Religion has been used as the great equalizer even before written religious doctrine. If God must threaten you to behave or believe, are your heart and soul on the path of enlightenment, or are you behaving out of fear of reprisals? Fear does not help raise your harmonic signature.

M: Not buying it, but what do you mean by your statement, "great equalizer"?

L: When you think about ancient times, who is it you picture ruling the clan, the tribe, a large group of people? Is it someone strong, intimidating, vicious when warranted, or do you imagine someone weak, intimidated, and passive?

M: I picture strength, a good fighter, intelligent, charismatic, a leader.

L: So how does the weak person who wants power and sway over people compete with this strong charismatic leader?

M: I suppose by using their knowledge of the gods, or a God, to sow fear and intimidation by threatening to ask said gods or God to punish nonbelievers.

L: Now the veil is lifting. There is nothing wrong with organized religion. For people to gather in like-mindedness for the betterment of themselves and others is necessary for some. That feeling of connection. But you must look closely for signs.

M: What kind of signs?

L: Individuals or groups who wield their religion like a club. Those that say they can absolve you of your sins in the name of God. That they speak for God or that God speaks through them. Have you ever wondered why God always speaks through men with few exceptions? In fact, many of the modern religions have marginalized females for thousands of years.

M: I can see that, but hasn't it always been the case?

L: Nope. Before modern religions came to prominence, many religious beliefs had both male and female deities, with a few exceptions. Today, most religious leaders are male, with females, while making progress, still remaining second-class citizens in two of the biggest religions on this planet, Christianity and Islam. In fact, many religions that had prominent female gods have been eradicated. Egyptian, Greek, Roman, Norse, Celtic, Aztec, and Sumerian, to name a few, all had powerful female goddesses revered by men and women alike. Now, it's one male God to rule the universe. It's priceless.

Research: I know of some ancient female deities like Venus, for instance, but I wanted to get a more complete picture of some of the main ones and discover how diverse and widespread they were in ancient times.

Celtic—Brigid is a revered goddess of spring and for her many talents. She is considered a protector of livestock and the young and is a patroness of poetry, metalsmithing, and healing.

Buddhist—Kaun Lin is the deity that embodies compassion and mercy and is dedicated to relieving the suffering in the world.

Egyptian—Isis is thought to be the most powerful of the Egyptian female deities. Mother of the god Horus, she is viewed as one of the most powerful of the Egyptian gods. Considered a protector, healer of the sick, and believed even powerful enough to bring the dead back to life, Isis was revered as a role model for mothers.

Hinduism—Shakti is the source from which all life springs, much like "Mother Earth" except viewed more like an energetic force or the underlying divine power of the universe.

Norse—Freya is known as the goddess of love and fertility. She also oversees the realm of Folkvang, where she helps guide the recently fallen, by her selection, to the afterlife.

Greek—Athena is the Greek goddess of wisdom. A goddess of poise and courage, she is also known as a lover of the arts and literature. She is the patron deity of Athens, and Athena was often called upon for protection and help with matters of governance.

Andean—Pachamama is revered as the Mother Earth goddess. She embodies nourishment and abundance, and she surrounds all of creation.

Buddhist—Mazu is the Chinese goddess of the sea.

Sumerian—Inanna is the goddess of sexual love and procreation, called the Queen of Heaven. She is often associated with the Mesopotamian goddess Ishtar and the Phoenician Astarte. She is also thought to be skilled in war and politics and is often depicted with lions to represent her courage and prowess.

Aztec—Coatlicue was the Aztec goddess who was the mother of the Aztec god of sun and war, Huitzilopochtli. In Aztec mythology, she also gave birth to the moon and stars.

Lucifer is not wrong. Many religions in the ancient past revered women as powerful deities. It's clear we have doctrines that spell out the path to a healthy soul and harmonic balance, so why the purposeful diminishing of the woman's place of power and influence? Something to explore further.

Let's Resume

Me: I can see how someone can look at it that way. I guess the question is, why?

Lucifer: Say you want influence, power, and control. You can try through force of arms, and many have, through the millennia, tried. But religion and force of arms can transcend borders, monarchies, and culture where pure might may not. It's a great equalizer. To rule through pure strength and charisma takes a skill set few humans possess. To rule through religion opens opportunities to all manner of men. You can add ideology as a form of religion as well.

Me: Example?

Lucifer: Oh, there are too many to count, but since we were just speaking about ancient religion, let's stick with that theme. Who has more sway over a hundred people? A man with a bat or a man who says he is a messenger of a God?

Me : I suppose the man with the bat can do more bodily damage.

Lucifer: You might think that. On the surface, the man with the bat is the most threatening—or is he? So you want an example. I'll give you a famous one: Thermopylae and the Spartans. The Spartans were touted as the world's best trained, disciplined, and vicious fighting force. When the Persians, with their million-man army, were on their way to attack Greece, the kings of Sparta wanted to mobilize their army. But unfortunately, the Persians were attacking during a religious observance called Carneia, which celebrated the god Apollo. The Spartan priests would not sanction the mobilization of the Spartan army during this observance. Instead, three hundred Spartans were allowed to escort King Leonidas as he mobilized a scouting party to gauge the Persian army's strength. The rest is history. Three hundred Spartans and 1,100 of their Greek allies held the Persian army at the gates of Thermopylae for three days before eventually being overwhelmed and destroyed. The consequence of the priests' decision was not only the loss of one of their beloved kings, Leonidas, but the delay allowed the Persians to flood into Greece and burn the Greek city of Athens to the ground.

M: I'm aware of this story.

L: This is just one of many examples of religious ego and power and its sway over powerful men eliciting dire consequences. We could get into humans' irrational acts of religious cleansing, ethnic cleansing, or outright class cleansing that have cost billions of souls over the millennia, but that is for another time.

Me: I would agree that very bad things have been done in the name of some god, gods or ideology, but incredibly good deeds have also been done. What is the true religion? Are you willing to tell me?

Lucifer: There are thousands of religions, all claiming to be the true path to whatever their version of heaven is. Thousands! All are claiming they are the true path to your soul's salvation. Many believe theirs is the only way, that any other belief is anywhere from ignorant or misguided to outright evil, and the practitioners of those religions must therefore be eradicated. Your species never disappoints. You are the same. Your souls are all connected. Yet, you try so hard to separate and isolate yourselves. Religion, gender, culture, skin tone, language, borders, ideology . . . You name it, and you'll use it. You have blue eyes, and I have green; therefore, you are bad, and I am good. It's wonderful and pathetic!

M: I concede we have our challenges, but there is so much good our species accounts for too. Religion, in its basic form, promotes community, faith, belief, continuity, accountability, and goodness. I find it interesting how you paint religion as a means of control. Yet, I see it as a place for support, guidance, and strength. I think religion scares you, and that's why you try so hard to diminish its influence.

L: Please, it does not scare me. The roots of most religions practiced here on earth are founded in the basic laws of the universe, as we discussed. Unfortunately, religion is often twisted, abused, and used for power and control. That is where you start to see how evil can take any idea, ideology, concept, or fact and manipulate it for its own gain if you are not diligent.

M: And if we are diligent?

L: Then evil will up its game to vilify it, cancel it, infiltrate it to undermine it, or deny it exists. Evil attacks anything that holds values of accountability. And accountability, at its core, is evil's, and even my, ultimate deterrent.

M: Accountable to whom? To ourselves, our souls? Our God's laws? The laws of the countries we live in? Truth? There is a lot to be accountable for.

L: That is true, but the laws of the universe are, well, universal. Again, it's accountability to the universe, God, the source, or the creator that is so hard for your species to wrap your heads around. It's your soul and its harmonic frequency and balance to the universe that you will ultimately be accountable to.

M: Can we get there?

L: Of course not, and it's why I'm here and not by God's side. Again, human souls are flawed and have been poisoned by greed and what seems like an endless need for destruction. You constantly seek ways to offend or be offended. To seek justice with a lack of justice. To irradicate racism with racism. To save the planet by destroying it. To willfully give power to an individual of low emotional intellect and low moral standards. You have become the masters of deflecting responsibility, blaming others for your actions, even knowing you have been gifted free will. It's convenient and lazy to blame others, even me, for your destructive behaviors. Yet, you have an army of apologists lined up to defend your actions or turn a blind eye in the name of being sympathetic, humane, or compassionate. It's pure condescension. You blame your bad behavior on the way you were brought up or the world in which you live but won't take ownership of the fact you are the master of your soul, the creator of the path you chose to walk, and an active participant in the world you live in. The road map is there to follow, but you make excuses, are ignorant, or worse, willfully ignorant of the truths. Or maybe it's as simple as you are just too lazy to walk the path to happiness, fulfillment, and enlightenment.

M: Just here in America, the country I live in, where you seem to take pleasure in trying to paint as some collection of degenerate souls, voluntarily contributed close to $430 billion to over a million nonprofit organizations here in the US. I believe one in four adults volunteer their time in some capacity. There is a lot of kindness and generosity in the world, more than there has been in recent history. You say there are thousands of religions. How wonderful is that! Thousands of religions trying to guide people to be better human beings. Maybe they all have it wrong or not exactly right, but they are trying to guide people to improve. Oh, I'm sure you can come up with hundreds of examples of religion gone bad, but I could probably come up with more examples of religion gone right.

L: True, there is a lot of kindness and generosity in the world. You must ask yourself two things: how much of it is genuine, and is there enough genuine kindness and generosity to tip the scales?

M: I guess you are referring to the notion expressed earlier about being unable to bribe, deceive, bully, or hide from your harmonic signature. That our genuine actions, good or bad, constantly tune our souls. Is there enough genuine goodwill to tip the scales in favor of a collective higher human harmonic signature? I don't know.

L: How much is being done to make this world a better place?

I will grant you that there are pockets of very good people doing good deeds, but the reason why you will lose the ultimate battle is doubt.

M: How so?

L: Everything we have discussed so far is in doubt because evil makes it so. Evil has infiltrated most institutions of power and influence to manipulate useful idiots in perpetuating ideology that is counter to the laws of the universe and the path of spiritual awakening, that it's laughable. My followers and I test, and the sheeple just follow along because they are too lazy to think for themselves.

M: Like when we discussed why Orthodox dogma won over Gnostic philosophy.

L: Yes, and this makes individuals easily manipulated and far too willing to set aside common sense. Or they profit from said ideology, gain power, popularity, or maybe all three. And gloriously, humans are absolutely willing to sacrifice their souls for instant gratification, fleeting fame, and the low probability of fortune. It's incredibly shortsighted and such a fertile ground for evil to prosper.

M: I want to focus on when you say, "your followers." Are you saying you have individuals who actually know you and follow you even though they understand they are dooming themselves into never joining the higher spiritual collective?

L: Let's just say I have spiritual influencers of a negative type.

Some of my best work is making people believe we don't even exist.

M: Your anti-Christ disciples, those dedicated to keeping us off the path?

L: Again, I am not anti-Christ, I am anti-Homo sapiens.

M: Are your followers demons? Do they possess people's minds and bodies? Corrupt their souls?

L: The devil made me do it? No, that would mean there would be no accountability. Because you are gifted free will, we entice, influence, deceive, and direct, but you ultimately own your choices that tune your harmonic frequency. We offer the apple; you decide if you will bite it.

M: What about mental illness?

L: What about it?

M: People with mental illness, how are they held accountable for their actions?

L: Remember, souls reincarnate or are placed here on earth to teach, some to test, and some to learn. People who have mental illness could be teachers, testers, or learners. Their souls will know and adjust their frequency accordingly.

M: Vague answer there.

L: Too complicated to explain. The universe is too complex

for humanity to comprehend fully. The path is simple. As I said, the Golden Rule, Ten Commandments, seven deadly sins, Buddhism, Confucianism, the Koran, Zoroastrianism, Proverbs and so many others... Take your pick. I mean, there is a lot of common sense floating around, and all can be traced to many different prior religions and beliefs, which, again, have the laws of the universe embedded in them. At their roots, they all lay out a good path for humanity to follow. You, Homo sapiens, tend to complicate things—secret teachings, cults, pseudo-science, blind faith, blind rejection, and shit. You have the potential to do all kinds of wonderful things. Powers you are only now starting to scratch the surface of. Humanity covets power too much, and the powerful are easy to manipulate because they don't want to lose what they have gained, even if it means selling their souls.

M: I believe that.

L: You should. I will also tell you this. So many countries, cultures, and societies throughout history, like America, have had the opportunity to elevate humanity. But I, like I have done for millennia, test. This experiment called America could have taken you, and the world, to a higher level of harmonic frequency.

M: So that's it. You recognize our potential as a nation, and you are destroying it from within.

L: Am I destroying it? I laugh in your face, victim. *You* are destroying it! I didn't force the apple into anyone's mouth. I will repeat myself. If the wealthy and powerful get people to look at everything through victimhood, get others to prop up victimhood through condescension disguised as compassion, suppress speech and debate by instituting censorship, keep the voting populous undereducated, willfully ignorant, angry, and easily manipulated, divide everyone by skin color, ethnicity, education, social class, gender, sex, religion, borders, etc., suppress free will, free speech, free thought, and do it all with deception, ego, and self-righteousness, you have a recipe for soul-crushing collapse. Ultimately, a one-world order, where 10 percent of the world's unelected elite control the other 90 percent . . . "for the good of the world".., How many civilizations have attempted a one-world order? Remember when we discussed one that soweth discord among brethren? The act most hated by God?

M: Yes.

L: Evil at its best. Think about humans with power and what they do with it, like big tech, big business, big pharma, government, media, higher education, cults, religion, content creators, adult influencers, teachers, and parents even. Many amass tremendous power, influence, and/or wealth by simply sowing discord amongst the populous. And it's everything from the color of your skin to the food you serve. A white-owned restaurant serving Mexican food is suddenly boycotted for cultural appropriation. A Hispanic man accused of a hate crime against a Black man is touted as a white supremacist because it fits a political narrative. It is the act most hated by God because it takes humanity off the path of enlightenment and harmonic balance in the guise of enlightenment and harmonic balance. When you sit back and watch these acts without prejudice or bias, you see the division, the hate, the deception, and the manipulation. And what is so delicious about it is the powerful get wealthier and more powerful while the useful idiots and their followers get their crumbs. Yet all get further and further away from true harmonic balance and enlightenment. They will all get screwed in the end.

M: So, it's the ignorant we should feel sorry for?

L: I'm not sure you should feel sorry for anyone. I mean, is ignorance an excuse? Again, teachers, testers, and learners. Only the soul really knows and will record accordingly.

M: So, our roles are predestined? Are they not self-determined?

L: Again, it's complicated, but let's say it's a mix. Your time, environment, parents, and other things may be predetermined, but your free will factors into outcomes. Sometimes, souls don't seem like they are given a chance to grow, but again, who ultimately judges that? As I stated, teachers, testers, and learners . . . All souls have a purpose each time they reincarnate into your existence.

M: To me, that is the big question. I look at aborted humans, children, and adults with mental and physical birth defects, mental illness, extreme and horrific living conditions, and think, how is that soul given a chance to grow? To bloom? To ascend? Why does God allow this?

L: What if their soul's growth depended on voluntary sacrifice to test and strengthen other souls? A willingness to live a life, no matter how brief or in how much suffering, just to allow others to test their compassion, selflessness, strength, resilience, kindness, sacrifice, or their lack of compassion, their selfishness, weakness, fragility, hatefulness, insecurity, and ego.

M: I imagine that would be quite the sacrifice and soul rewarding. To endure such hardships for the advancement of others and themselves.

L: Yes, well, I look at it differently, of course. I feel their sacrifices really highlight how incredibly self-absorbed, shitty, and contrary your species can be.

M: Contrary?

L: Yeah, contrary. Let me give you an example. "*I've got two daughters—nine and six years old. I'm going to teach them first of all about values and morals. But I don't want them punished with a baby if they make a mistake. I don't want them punished with an STD at sixteen.*"—President Obama. At the time, arguably, the most powerful individual on the planet.

In contrast:

"*I feel the greatest destroyer of peace today is 'Abortion' because it is a war against the child . . . A direct killing of the innocent child, 'Murder' by the mother herself . . . And if we can accept that a mother can kill even her own child, how can we tell other people not to kill one another? How do we persuade a woman not to have an abortion? As always, we must persuade her with love . . . And we remind ourselves that love means to be willing to give until it hurts . . .*"—Mother Teresa.

Two powerful influencers with two very different messages. Words matter. Which influencer do you think creates the most positive egregore?

M: Egregore? Please explain what the heck that is.

L: Today, it simply means a group of like-minded people with common motivations influenced by an individual or group of collective people.

M: So, in your example, President Obama is the leader or at least a key influencer of a group of like-minded individuals, and they are part of his egregore?

L: Correct, and Mother Teresa has her egregore, and there are countless egregores. What do you hope to achieve by sharing this conversation with other people? Create an egregore yourself, correct?

M: I guess. I set out to challenge, understand, and enlighten myself by seeking truth or maybe just clear the lens through which I view myself and the world. I share our conversation with the same intention. Nothing I share is with the belief the science is settled. I share my journey with the hope that others will either start, continue, and/or share theirs. Like you said earlier, 20 percent of readers will connect, 60 percent will consider some of this conversation as interesting, and 20 percent will absolutely reject everything presented in this conversation.

L: It's the first 20 percent that become part of your groupthink, your tribe. More depending on how many neutral readers, doing their own journey, as you say, come to many of your same conclusions. So, let's circle back to the two influencers, Mother Teresa and President Obama. Which one has a higher frequency message?

M: If I break it down simply, one advocates putting oneself before others, and one advocates putting others before oneself. Seems obvious.

L: Do you think putting others before yourself is always good? If a person belongs to a group, and that group advocates for something against his beliefs, but he goes along, is he putting others before himself? You seem to want to break things down too simple, and, to you, obvious outcomes. But your existence is more complex than you can possibly comprehend; yet, it can be so simple if you choose.

M: How's this for simple, when someone habitually places themselves before others, lacks accountability, and/or advocates against accountability for one's actions, is selfish, egotistical, lacks grace, and is deceptive, both in rhetoric and/or deeds? That person willingly, or in ignorance, is doing your work.

L: Some of my work. But remember, I want your total destruction. It's evil who wants to subjugate you.

Brief Summary: I'll pause here to summarize my thoughts so far, with more conversation to come. First, evil is a con game. It entices, even preys on the duality within all of us. And there is true evil out there, and true evil does not want humanity to evolve spiritually. It feeds and profits off negative energy. It's okay to lie for the greater good, murder for the greater good, and sow dissension for the greater good. Evil wants you to believe there are no consequences or that the consequences of bad for good will ultimately lead to good. It seeks to discredit the "path" to our soul's harmonic balance and to stop our ascension to the universal collective. Simply, evil tries to stop us from simply being decent human beings. All for power, control, vanity, ego, and/or wealth.

The thing is, I know I have behaved in ignorance or in full knowledge of actions that have negatively impacted others as well as me. This project has been years in the making and certainly life-changing. I've learned so much and had so many unexpected questions, all of which have given me pause to rethink how I connect with, evaluate, and react too, everything. Harmonic balance with the universe? Ascension? Many of these concepts are a bit outside my pay grade, as they say. But I'm trying to understand. Regardless of what we choose to believe, want to believe, or even reject, we must do better and be better. I hope you have been challenged so far and have done your own research and soul-searching. Like a snowflake, our journey can be a beautiful thing, but like a snowflake, no two journeys can be identical. It's my hope your destination will be as rewarding to you as mine has been so far for me. Thanks for coming along this far. I hope you continue because there is more to contemplate, maybe get upset about, refute, or embrace. So, let's resume if you're willing.

The Discussion Resumes

Me: Okay, so the path is laid out for us. And we have influencers who try to guide us along the path, and influencers, complicit or in ignorance, enticing us off the path. And you, putting in all this work just to prove God is wrong about us. Seems petty and beneath a being of your enlightenment and stature.

Lucifer: Petty? I don't operate in pettiness. I have a clear objective, and I have patience. You think you know God? The God of the Old Testament who demands blood sacrifice, or the God of the New Testament who asks you to turn the other cheek? The wrathful God or the just God? Maybe you have no idea who God really is.

Me: Possibly. I think we agreed earlier that God is the creator and has given us directions on how to live a life that helps us evolve our life force, our harmonic frequency. We have the Ten Commandments, the Golden Rule, and the seven deadly sins, among so many other guides. Seems straightforward.

Lucifer: Straightforward, yes. But it seems like such a narrow path you're so easily nudged off is the point we keep circling around. Take the seven deadly sins, as you call them—lust or extravagance, gluttony, greed, sloth, wrath, envy, and pride. Take lust, for example. Let's say greed, cravings, excitement, lewdness, and carnality are embedded in it. What quickly comes to mind when you think of lust?

Me: The first things that come to mind are money, rape, pedophilia, unfaithfulness, and lack of impulse control. Money for greed, rape for carnality, pedophilia for cravings, unfaithfulness for excitement, and lack of impulse control for lewdness.

Lucifer: And gluttony?

M: Excess, consuming or hoarding more than needed. I always think of those individuals that bought thousands of dollars' worth of toilet paper when the pandemic first broke out, not caring if others had to go without.

L: Toilet paper? That's an inconvenience, now baby formula, hording that during a severe shortage, that is humanity at its finest. Take that act you just described for example. A little strife and scare mongering and many people became incredibly selfish and self-serving. Easily manipulated. Now, how do you keep people in this low vibrational state?

M: You continue to feed the machine.

L: Correct. Now, let's stay on topic, another part of gluttony you did not mention and it's what many people think when you reference gluttony is eating in excess, leading to obesity. Many are afraid to talk about the effects of being overweight for fear of being accused of fat shaming. I love it. Keep empowering unhealthy behaviors. Have you ever heard of, or known a 90-year-old obese person? Many deaths from COVID19 were the consequence of people who were obese and unhealthy.

M: Where are you going with this? I think there is a big difference between people who work out regularly but are larger built versus individuals who are unhealthy and obese.

L: Of course, but here is where I'm going with this. The media and influencers had a large portion of your countries populous believing 50% of people hospitalized with COVID died. Again, I love the media and I love stupid people. Corruption, manipulation, and stupidity. The approximate numbers are less than 1% of people that were hospitalized with COVID died and 75% of the deaths were people over 65 or "overweight" and/or with pre-existing health concerns or illnesses.

M: I concede the media does create a steady stream of strife and fear, manufactured or real. They perpetuate low frequency behaviors. And unfortunately, from our discussions, low frequency behaviors stymie our spiritual growth.

L: Behaviors like greed. Think of all the lies that prop up strife and scare mongering. Most of the print and television news use these tactics for profit, power, and fame. Politics as well. So many politicians, broadcasters, news reporters, and editors display no shame, either. If you pay attention, media uses phrases like undisclosed sources, reliable sources, there is a good chance or, it's probable. These phrases are meant to project their narrative solely to gain viewers, get clicks, sway viewers, or get votes, regardless of the facts or context. It's deceptive but packaged in a way so they don't have to own it or be accountable. The question is, who is worse . . . the seller or the consumer?

M: I would say the seller as they knowingly peddle half-truths, conjecture as truth, or falsehoods for gain. Sowing discord amongst brethren is the one act most detested by God. But interestingly, you have brought up the consumer. Sloth is one of the deadly sins we haven't covered yet. Is it wrong to be lazy about the information you take as truth without verifying its validity? And what about passing it along to others? And these egregores, this group-think mentality, how many members just follow along to belong? How many are lazy and just go along because it's easier than exploring alternative ideas? How many people are scared not to go along for fear of cancelation, ridicule, or lost friendships?

L: Now, let's add another deadly sin, wrath, into that web of chaos. Oh, how the weak are easily seduced into anger, fury, and outrage. Righteous indignation!

M: Rage, cancel culture, defamation, revenge, and I could go on, but to me, it is easy to see why wrath is considered a deadly sin. I'm willing to wrap it up with envy, which ties into many of these sins, along with pride, the worst of the deadly sins and one you seem to have an abundance of.

L: Pride? I'm superior to you in every way. Spiritually, intellectually, and physically. It's not pride; it's truth. Pride in humans . . . *that* is priceless. You are so underwhelming, so petty, so unwilling to be decent that I laugh at your "pride." You disgust me in your ignorance or willful ignorance. Oh, not in your ignorance of the universe and its workings. That is beyond your ability to grasp at this point in your development. No, you disgust me because of your willful ignorance. Your desire to be right and your pride and ego prevent you from admitting you were wrong. The pride you have in knowing you have all the answers and the lack of humility to make sure what you know is correct. Your willingness to quickly pick a side and dogged determination to stay the course even when the mounting evidence is not on your side.

M: Broad brush there. I believe many humans have plenty of humility and are absolute seekers of truth. Pride is a deadly sin without humility, but together, you have confidence, an open mind, and a willingness to learn. It seems to me pride, ego, and lack of humility lead to our soul's devolution.

L: Maybe, but humility can hold people back. With very little humility, I shape the thoughts and minds of the masses. Try to find a leader with humility, pride, and ego. Not many. It's why I've been so successful at burning both ends of the candle.

M: How so?

L: I'm the prince of chaos, among other titles. Chaos is the catalyst or maybe the result of my work. Sometimes, chaos works for humanity's benefit, but most of the time, it's to its detriment. You want simple; I want complicated chaos. For instance, I would say any sane society wants clean air to breathe, clean water to drink, and clean food to eat while living in peace and safety with their loved ones. I would add to those simple things like loving who you choose in peace, raising a family safely if you so choose, and living fulfilled lives. Is there anything here you would disagree with?

M: No, I think those are all good things.

L: I agree, so why is it so damn difficult to get the human species to agree? Chaos? I contend it's unreasonable, egocentric, prideful, and evil humans.

M: Evil?

L: That's right. Evil and psychotic humans of influence who prey on the weak-minded masses who lack or reject common sense.

M: And you just love evil, don't you?

L: I detest evil. Evil is why I don't want you in the universal collective. I create challenges, and humanity either rises or falls to those challenges. And every time you fail, you feed negative entities, the negative parasites that inhabit this earthly realm. They grow in power and influence. Oh, I know you think it's me, but I'm quite forthcoming in my desire to see you fail. Evil is secretive, diabolical, manipulative, and hungry.

M: So why are you different than evil?

L: I don't want to rule you; evil does. Evil wants you to fall; I want you to fail. I want you to destroy yourselves. Evil does not want you to destroy yourselves; it wants to rule, manipulate, control, and subjugate. Look back at all the subjects we've covered. I test, you fail, and evil grows as humanity loses its soul.

M: I think you're full of shit. Evil achieves your goals, doesn't it? Humanity's demise is your goal, and it seems to me evil helps that cause greatly, if not entirely.

L: Can you not destroy the world without evil?

M: Give me an example.

L: Let's say COVID was indeed lab created, which, believe it or not, is likely. But the scientists didn't create it out of evil.

Yet, it accidentally got into the population, causing death and chaos. Now, evil took advantage but was not the catalyst. Evil never lets crises go to waste. People suffer while evil gains power, wealth, and influence. Without the easily manipulated, how does evil stay in power? Evil would have to eat its own; eventually, nothing remains. No, evil needs people to feed off.

M: I guess you're right now that I think about it. Humanity can be ignorant, stupid even, and know not what they do. They can destroy the planet without being evil, so I get your point.

L: And free will does not coincide with common sense. Evil struggles against common sense. Again, evil thrives on chaos. It seeks out controversy and throws kerosene on the fire. It warps common sense and exploits people to carry out its agenda without them even realizing they are evil's tools. When you kill common sense, you control the masses.

M: The Commandments, deadly sins, and Golden Rule are all founded on common sense, both for a healthy society and a healthy soul. Take care of your mind, body, and soul, and all will be right, right?

L: Yes, but it's so hard, isn't it? It's so easy for you to fail and then blame others for that failure. It's so easy to fall from grace yet view it as success. People reject common sense because it holds them accountable.

M: Common sense by whose standards?

L: The universe's.

M: And that's the problem, isn't it? The universal standard is so simple, yet we humans can't embrace it or find balance. We need antagonists; we need an enemy; we create chaos. As Elon Musk famously said in 2022, "Do we want a humorless society that is simply rife with condemnation and hate? At its heart, wokeness is divisive, exclusionary, and hateful. It basically gives mean people . . . a shield to be mean and cruel, armored in false virtue." It doesn't matter if you like Elon Musk. That quote encapsulates how out of balance we are as a species. Yet, as we evolve in technology, it seems we are devolving harmonically.

L: Yes, the easier life is, the less things are appreciated. Have you heard the following?

My grandfather walked ten miles to work every day. My father walked five miles to work every day. I drive a Cadillac to work, and my son is in a Mercedes. My grandson will be in a Ferrari, but my great-grandson will be walking again . . . Do you want to know why?

Because . . .

Tough Times create Strong Men; Strong Men create Easy Times; Easy Times create Weak Men; Weak Men create Tough Times.

M: We are in easy times.

L: Easy times, yes, but you're rapidly headed toward very hard times, and it's evil at the helm. Take a minute to reflect on the chaos around you. Really reflect and tell me if it makes any common sense.

M: One of the biggest things in the news in the last couple of years is *Roe v. Wade* and abortion rights. We touched on this before, and you said, "It's the most destructive to one's harmonic signature."

L: I did, and it is.

M: You don't believe in a woman's right to choose? In a woman's reproductive rights?

L: I couldn't give two shits what humans do with your bodies. But look at it from the viewpoint of evil, ignorance, and hypocriticalness. How do *you* feel about abortion?

M: I believe in the woman's right to choose, but I also think abortion is destructive. I prefer men and women protect themselves from unwanted pregnancy or, if it does happen, have the baby. But I also believe there should be safe places for women to have abortions if they want one. All these choices are free will, accountability of one's soul, and the consequences of one's actions. So I don't think my view is evil, ignorant, or hypocritical.

L: You're a fence rider. Either you believe in the sanctity of life, or you don't. You're weak.

M: Fuck off. It's a commonsense stance.

L: Really? Let's unpack your "common sense." Can we agree that Planned Parenthood is the number one performer of abortions in the United States?

M: We can agree on that.

Research: According to the Pew Research Center 2020, clinics made up 50 percent of abortion providers in 2020, but they administered 96 percent of all abortions that year (54 percent in abortion clinics and 43 percent in other clinics).

L: Can we also agree that the creator of Planned Parenthood, Margret Sanger, created the organization under pretenses that could be considered evil?

M: Yes, she was quite open about creating Planned Parenthood to advance eugenics, which is incredibly racist and a doctrine that supports white supremacy.

L: Wrap your head around this. According to your CDC, just in 2019, abortion rates by race in the US are as follows:

- White: 33 percent; 6.6 abortions per 1,000 women.

- Black: 38 percent; 23.8 abortions per 1,000 women.

- Hispanic: 21 percent; 11.7 abortions per 1,000 women.

- Other: 7 percent; 13 abortions per 1,000 women.

Margret Sanger created a for-profit company to advance eugenics that still performs her intended work today. Evil just flipped the script from eugenics and white supremacy to "woman's right to choose" and "women's reproductive health." It's all how you package it, but the results are the same. If you really want to twist yourself up, compare it to another hot debate that the US was founded on slavery and racism, and it is woven systemically into the culture of the US.

M: How do you possibly conflate the two?

L: The same people that decry that America was founded on slavery and white supremacy, which is woven systemically into the US culture, are typically the same people who will fight for an organization that was designed to, and is systemically still, performing the work its founder, Margret Sanger, intended it for. Are people evil, ignorant, or disingenuous?

M: I think people have good intentions and genuinely believe they are trying to improve people's lives and this planet.

L: I will counter that more people are comfortable tearing down than building up. I mean, how interesting that the party of white supremacy and replacement theory is "pro-life," and the party of supposed inclusivity, equality, and tolerance is "pro-choice"? Evil is the master of making white seem black, and black seem white. I mean, seriously, I watch pro-choice advocates call pro-life advocates racist and absolutely believe what they are saying. People protest, intimidate, and vandalize pro-life clinics. All these clinics do is offer women choices to abortion. As a species, you're so fucking stupid. Why can't the two coexist, and what is so wrong with believing abortion should be the last resort versus the first?

M: You're the master of duplicity and lies.

L: Oh, I am, but I thought the whole exercise of this conversation was to challenge what you think you know. So, prove I'm wrong. In fact, I'll go one step further down this rabbit hole just to throw more doubt on what you think you know because

I like it. How many pro-choice people are white supremacists? How many are racist without anyone knowing? How many believe stupid people breed stupid people and, therefore, should terminate their potential—no, eventual—burden on society? How many in the government? In media? And if not supremacists themselves, unwitting stooges? Who owns the media? White men? Who are the most aggressive advocates for abortion? White women? Who, by the way, are statistically less likely to have an abortion than any other race in America, according to the CDC?

M: Again, you are the problem, creating chaos with conspiracy theories. That's your MO, whispering conspiracy theories, innuendos, and lies. A woman should absolutely have the right to choose what she does with her body.

L: They should. But think about that choice. To terminate a potential life, a soul, that delays its chance to realize its potential. There is so much debate in trying to define when life begins. Why is that? Is it because most people have a conscience and therefore feel better about terminating a blob of cells rather than an unborn child? Just call it like it is. The potential of life begins at conception, and abortion ends that life's potential. And we covered how some souls reincarnate to test, teach, and/or learn, yes?

M: Yes.

L: How do you think an unborn child tests one's soul?

M: Now that you ask, a few scenarios come to mind. Take a

woman who starts dating a guy and gets pregnant. She is a young entrepreneur with a very successful business. She lets her new boyfriend know she is pregnant, and he lets her know he fully intends to be involved with raising the child. Nevertheless, she decides on her own to terminate the pregnancy without consulting him because she is not ready to have the child, even though the boyfriend in this scenario may be willing to raise the baby on his own without her assistance. Granted, she did not plan on getting pregnant. She might even have tried to protect herself, and the contraception failed. The pregnancy, nevertheless, occurred, and she had choices to make. The choice to terminate the pregnancy without exploring other available options may have profound adverse effects on her soul's harmonic signature, or it may not.

L: And the second one?

M: A couple's firstborn was a difficult pregnancy, but they decided to have a second child, only to discover while the baby was in the womb, the baby had a rare and life-limiting condition. The baby would not be able to develop fully and, therefore, will only survive outside the womb for a very short time . . . hours only. The couple, devastated, discussed all their options, including abortion. Finally, after much discussion and soul searching, they decided to have the baby, even though there was a chance of complications for the mother. They made this difficult decision because they wanted the baby to know, even briefly, that the baby was loved and would always be a part of their family. Two pregnancies, two different decisions, two different impacts on the soul.

L: Why do you say it's possible the abortion performed in your first story "may" have profound adverse effects on her soul?

M: I'm not her soul's judge, right? Her soul is. I only know what I know about the situation, and there is undoubtedly an amount of conjecture. But as we discussed, only her soul knows the ultimate effect, and it can't be bribed, tricked, bullied, or lied to, right?

L: That is right. Every soul has a mission, a reason for being here on earth, a destiny. In your second story, maybe the baby was placed in the couple's path to help them understand or even test their unconditional and selfless love. Even in the first scenario, what if the woman later in life had another opportunity to have a baby but this time, was so grateful for a second chance, she cherished this child and was a better mother for it? Maybe there was another reason. But to your point, who can say? Not all destinies are realized or fulfilled.

M: Is that because of free will?

L: Free will, influencers, ignorance, fear, SAD.

M: Situational Awareness Disorder?

L: Yes, and as we discussed before, egregores.

M: Like yours.

L: Again, mine or evil's? People primarily learn in three ways. They learn from a leader they trust, from experience, or through research and study.

M: So do you blame evil for what abortion has come to, or will you take some ownership?

L: Humanity embracing the act of systematically exterminating its future, yeah, I can live with ownership to protect the universe from the plague I call humanity.

M: Commit evil to combat evil? A bad deed for the greater good?

L: Again, is abortion evil, or is abortion just a woman's right to choose what she does with her body?

M: It can be both. It all comes down to motivation, doesn't it? So what are the reasons you're for it? Because you want population control and to hold power over others, or because there are legitimate and deeply profound reasons for an abortion to be performed?

L: You view it as evil? Was fighting Hitler and stopping Nazi Germany from taking over the planet evil? I view humanity the way most humans view Hitler and his Nazi regime. Evil, scary, and flawed. As I've said, evil acts sow the seeds of division and chaos for personal satisfaction, power, and gain. What evil always lacks is gratitude. Genuine gratitude.

M: Gratitude? Based on that definition, many people would fall into the evil category.

L: No. Evil people always lack the concept of genuine gratitude. Not all people who lack gratitude are evil.

M: That's a slippery slope and a huge assumption.

L: I'm not asking you to believe me. I'm just telling you what I know. Evil can feel satisfaction, sure, but gratitude is not in evil's wheelhouse.

M: So, if I understand you, you see yourself as the universe's savior by enticing humanity off its God-given path, or at the very least, showing us an alternative path that has us operating our existence at such low frequencies as never to be able to evolve and be accepted into the universal collective.

L: Correct

M: Evil, which you profess to detest, and humanity blames you for, or I should say, credits you with evil's introduction to humanity, has a mission to actively lower our harmonic frequency to a state that will prevent us from realizing a more enlightened state of being. Also, you seem to suggest that evil is an entity. A life force of its own, right?

L: It is taught in most religious teachings that I am, or some concept of me, is the entity of evil and that practitioners of evil worship me in one form or another. The reality is good and evil both reside in the duality of humans. I test, remember? Now, an individual who embraces evil can be a leader, influencer, or teacher of evil, and people of free will can follow or reject evil. Free will, as with good and evil, reside in most humans.

M: So, evil can be learned.

L: It can be learned, indoctrinated, embraced, propagated, and fermented. The question is, can it be forgiven, as many religions say they have the power to do?

M: Is that a rhetorical question?

L: I'm asking you what you think.

M: You can change and raise your soul's harmonic frequency with good thoughts and deeds, but to be forgiven is a fallacy propagated by evil. To behave with evil intent all your life just to have all forgiven in the end relieves humanity of consequence and responsibility for their behavior. It also garners power to those who espouse their ability to forgive your evil and sin.

L: Lead or participate in evil without fear of consequence? No, you give them too much credit. They don't believe in salvation, or maybe they don't put much thought into salvation when they are participating in evil acts or living a life of evil intent for the gains we discussed earlier. Evil does not have a conscience. Now, people that do evil acts are not necessarily evil. Remember, to sin is to miss the mark, and over time, people who are consistently committed to improving their aim evolve toward a more enlightened life. But what evil people are good at is redefining what evil acts are.

M: Like abortion and when life begins in the womb.

L: That is two of many. Take gender as another example. You are now blurring the lines of what a man and a woman are. A biological man can give birth? Is it now a birthing person in place of a mother? Are people trying to normalize multiple personalities, or are they just accommodating gender dysphoria? I mean, on the surface, who gives a shit, except now, biological males can identify as women with access to places and things they could not before. Or at least they couldn't without possible consequences. Now, they want access to woman's restrooms, locker rooms, and sports just because they identify as a woman and are not comfortable in a man's world. But have all the women who championed this new reality ever considered it's just another way men continue to impose their will and power over women? There is no uproar about trans men wanting to play men's sports or enter men's locker rooms or restrooms. No, it's biological men who are demanding the right to be a woman, with all the privileges that go with it. The goalposts are moved, and definitions are changed. If you're a dad and you speak out expressing you don't want your teenage daughter exposed to men's genitalia in the woman's locker room at school, even though the biological male says he identifies as a woman, chances are you will be vilified.

If you're a biological female athlete who objects to a trans woman in your locker room, you're asked to attend transgender sensitivity training. It's so awesome to watch men concede more and more power to women just to find new inventive ways to take it back. It's horrible now to think biological women might not be comfortable with men's genitalia being exposed in their once private sanctums. And now, you even have trans women upset because they say they are gay and can't understand why gay women won't date them. It's like the feminist movement has its eyes wide shut and bowing down to men.

M: I have compassion for those genuinely suffering from

gender dysphoria. I can't imagine the struggles they go through. However, I can't get behind in supporting gender transitioning for minors. Doctors, counselors, psychologists, psychiatrists, and parents, please, just stop. Give them emotional and clinical support until they are old enough to make these permanent life-altering decisions for themselves. I mean, unless you think not only is a child cognitively advanced enough to make these life-altering decisions about their sex, but they are also advanced enough to make decisions on smoking, drugs, alcohol, permanent tattoos, sex with adults, starting a family, voting, driving, and the need for education. There is a line in a movie I heard that I think is appropriate here, "What is with all the fuckery?"

L: Yeah, here is another quite famous quote or something close to it. "You need a license to buy a dog, a license to drive, hell, you even need a license to catch a fish, but any asshole can be a parent."

M: Close.

L: Some parents are raising weak, entitled, and empowered kids.

M: And you going to tell me evil takes advantage?

L: Oh, it does, and pedophilia is evil's cauldron. Hypersexualizing children is one of the fundamental tenants of evil's grasp on power. Child trafficking, pornography, molestation, grooming, and exploitation do so much long-lasting damage to all victims of such actions and those who perpetuate, promote, participate in, and forgive such acts. Your species is so fucking damaged you don't even pursue offenders in power unless it is right in your face. There is nothing to see here, people, because he will end fossil fuels and save the planet. Take Jeffery Epstein and his suspicious "suicide," where the surveillance cameras conveniently went inoperable at the time of his death. Or his business associate Ghislaine Maxwell who was convicted of underage sex trafficking and sentenced to 20 years in prison. She had all the names of visitors to Jeffery Epstein's island over the years, the alleged enclave of underaged sex trafficking. What happened to the documentation? What about Jeffery Epstein's suspicious suicide, and why has mainstream media coverage evaporated with a few exceptions? Where is the demand by Congress to see this list? Why did Twitter censor "@TrackerTrial," an account monitoring Maxwell's trial? The account was two weeks old and had 525,000 followers before it was suspended.

M: I'm not sure why, but on the surface, it seems like many powerful people doing evil acts have suppressed what should have been an explosive story that would hold horrible people accountable for terrible behavior.

L: That island tested a lot of souls. Business leaders, politicians, celebrities, the wealthy and connected, as well as the exploited.

M: Seeing people get away with so much crime and corruption is frustrating. I mean, look at our last few presidents. Creepy, childish, vindictive, deceptive, destructive, and corrupt.

L: And how fucking sad is that? In a country of over 300 million people, you landed on those candidates? I mean, some are mostly just assholes, but others are unfathomable. Few people know who they really are. Men of 1,000 faces, and many in your country choose to ignore it. Of course, they see it, but they don't care as long as they get their wants met. People will embrace the suck if they think their issue or issues will be advanced. There were a lot of decent, commonsense presidential candidates on all sides. Who wanted these candidates to lose? Who profits from the chaos, division, anger, and distrust? The media. The RNC, the DNC, and the media are run by whom? The special interest groups are run by whom? And the media sheep have no moral fiber to push back and do real investigative work to vet and back a decent person. I love it! You're shit.

M: You paint such a bleak picture, but there is an extensive populous of grounded, commonsense individuals who are more balanced toward service for others than service for self. We might not see it as we are overwhelmed by the "me" and "get mine" culture that constantly seems to be in our faces, but they are there.

L: Let's circle back to evil and its modus operandi, shall we? Evil acts sow the seeds of division and chaos for personal satisfaction, power, and greed. There is little room for honesty and integrity. Humans need to be honest with themselves. I mean, truly honest, and sometimes, it will be ugly. The biggest liar is often the person staring right back at you in the mirror. You are constantly underplaying the importance of honesty. You constantly bend, shape, abstract, and manipulate the truth to fit your comfort. And lack of integrity seems to be more acceptable; yet there is so much intolerance. And evil is so incredibly adept at making facts and things you see with your own eyes and hear with your ear unbelievable. You might witness a crime, have friends, colleagues, and family members victims of crime, and statistics showing crime in your city is on the rise, but evil . . . Evil will make you believe that those things are not real. That they know the actual facts and to trust them. Don't trust your eyes, your ears, or the facts. I will tell you what to believe.

M: I agree with that. I think about the defund the police movement. Society wants to hold the police to the highest standards of behavioral perfection. Yet, society is held to a lower and lower standard of behavior. The police—love them or hate them—are the bedrock of a healthy society. Without them, evil has no deterrent, and we see this play out worldwide.

L: Destroy the rule of law, and chaos follows.

M: Or control law enforcement and rule with an iron fist. Weaponize law enforcement to quell your opposition. It is what evil has done for millennia.

L: Destroy public confidence in the police and any authority, and then have the government take control for the good of the people. It's quite diabolical, and you see it take hold in your own country. Defund the police movement came on the heels of the BLM movement. With the help of the media and influencers, people of color distrust law enforcement. In addition, the white population is also losing trust, but, of course, the facts don't support this manufactured mistrust.

M: I have a friend who is high up in law enforcement, and they have a hard time recruiting to fill spots vacated by early retirement or those that simply left the force because of the fear and abuse they and their families had to endure daily. Society has less and less respect for law enforcement and goes out of its way to provoke, resist, and be combative with the hopes of a lawsuit or getting someone fired. It's becoming a slippery slope, in my opinion. Like politics, the nastier it becomes, the less attractive it becomes for decent people. So you are left with individuals who don't care what other people think and are only out for themselves, their ego, and their power over others.

L: Some say it's the unintended consequences of what started as a good cause. But never underestimate the calculation, the patience, and the manipulation of evil. While I detest it, I certainly respect it and even applaud it.

M: You keep saying you detest evil, but please, you are the prince of lies and the father of evil.

L: So religions say. Whether or not you believe me is of no consequence. It does not diminish evil's impact on humanity's souls. It's the fight for souls that is raging, and evil does not fight fair. I give you choices, but evil wants to take away choices.

M: Based on that analysis, one could argue pro-choice is good and pro-life is evil given the fact that pro-lifers want to make abortion illegal and take away the choice.

L: Some do, but others just want more education and awareness of available options. Remember, evil influences the weak mind and the greedy heart. Imagine an evolved society that advocates for the mutilation of children. We see it in third world countries that mutilate young girls' genitals so that they remain pure until their husband consummates the marriage. Most sane people find this barbaric. But if a young male child decides they feel like they are a girl, you will inevitably find adults who will condone placing their own child on puberty blockers and even agree to gender reassignment surgery. Why stop there? As you said earlier, if you are saying a young child knows what is best for them at such a young age, why not let them drink alcohol, smoke, take drugs, have sex with an adult, drive, and vote? I mean, you are saying they are mature enough to make a decision that will affect the rest of their life—irreversible decisions. Damn, your species has some sick people in it.

M: I think people start off meaning well but lose their common sense as they get caught up in the bright lights. I remember being young and stupid, doing dumb things that I thought would make me popular or fit in. Today, you almost have celebrity status if you're gay or transgender. Other kids want to be your friend because they don't want to be called homophobic or transphobic. Kids might not even like you because you're an asshole, but they are afraid to say it out loud for fear of being called a homophobe or transphobe and "canceled." Kids walking around with victim privilege, drumming up drama to maintain their victim card. And adults play along, encouraging it and enabling it.

L: Is it wrong?

M: Being transgender? No, if that is what you truly are. Living your true self in peace and harmony with your soul can only be good. But being in constant victim status can't be soul rewarding, no matter the circumstances, can it? I mean, how can you evolve mentally, physically, and spiritually if you are constantly angry, fearful, spiteful, hateful, sad, downtrodden, and suppressed? Now, I'm not saying those feelings are not all legitimate. We all struggle with those feelings occasionally without the extra burdens associated with gender dysphoria. But if it is manufactured for self-righteousness, subterfuge, and/or to belong, the vibrational frequency and the impact on the soul must be profoundly damaging.

L: That is all true. Evil is most definitely driving some of those feelings, and I have no small part in offering choices that create those feelings as well. The difference is, I give you free will to choose your path but often, evil suppresses free will, forcing those states upon you. And let's not underestimate the power of humans' incessant need to belong. Humans will perform all manner of corruption or violence, or take up the lowest vibrational causes, just to belong. And evil has empowered the weakest minds and souls to create egregores for the sheep to join and defend.

M: That's true. I just read about a movement to normalize pedophilia. A professor who wrote a book titled *A Long, Dark Road: Minor-Attracted People and Their Pursuit for Dignity*. This professor champions that the label "pedophile" has an unfair stigma attached to it, and the more acceptable designation should be "minor-attracted person." What is interesting is that Old Dominion University forced this professor out of their school, yet Johns Hopkins turned around and hired this controversial professor. I cannot think of a more reprehensible act than adults taking advantage of the young and innocent.

L: Controlling, manipulating, exploiting, and indoctrinating children, as I said, is evil's playbook. Child trafficking, hyper sexualization in the name of education and inclusivity, pedophilia, even eugenics, and let's throw in the selling of fetal tissue and stem cells of aborted babies for profit, can all be listed under the category of the adult's exploitation of the innocent and vulnerable. Evil must erode universal truths and norms by making lying, stealing, murder, disrespect, family disintegration, unhealthiness, greed, laziness, victimhood, and lack of accountability more acceptable. And the rejection of those behaviors shows a lack of empathy, grace, love, and forgiveness. I will continue to point out that making red, blue, or black, white, or green, purple, is what evil does.

M: Yeah, evil seems to suppress common sense for many people. I mean, when you start trying to mainstream the label "minor-attracted people," and society starts to conform, you are in trouble as a species, I will grant you that. But I believe that all the subjects we've discussed are really values of a loud minority and not embraced by the silent majority.

L: But it is the silent majority that allows evil to spread, corrupt, thrive, and metastasize into the very fabric of your species' soul. It's why I despise you.

M: You despise us because we are not perfect? That we are not evolving fast enough? That we are flawed?

L: No. I despise your kind because of the gifts bestowed upon you and your weakness in not taking advantage of them.

M: Well, you don't make it fucking easy, now, do you? What about *your* weakness, *your* flaws, *your* lack of evolution? It seems to me that if you were so evolved, you would be more like Jesus, Buddha, Confucius, Asha, or the Creator, if you like. But you are not. You stifle growth and damage souls. So to me, you are not an enlightened being.

L: What if my mission is to cull the dark souls from the rest? To ensure the low frequency, weak, and corrupt souls are tested and exposed? What if this was God's assignment given to me? You think you know so much, yet you know so little about how our infinite universe works. Maybe your planet is one of many inhabited planets, and all souls in this dimension are tested. Think of your soul as a battery. Negative energy drains the soul, and positive energy charges the soul, and you need an abundance of positive energy to ascend to a higher plane of being, of consciousness. So, it stands to reason that your battery eventually dies if you live your life off the path in negativity and don't recharge it with more positive energy than the negative energy you use. Your soul eventually dies. Take you, for example.

M: Okay.

L: Where do you think your soul is? Do you love more than you hate? Do you give more than you take? Do you expend more negative energy than you replenish with positive? Is the world better for having you in it?

M: I would like to think I'm of added value, but I am also humble enough to know I have a long way to go.

L: You don't know, is the point. But it's that willingness to be better, explore, find the path, and accept it as a journey. But you don't have infinite time to get to your destination. It's finite, or there would be no consequences to existing in darkness and low frequency. I'm the tester. I give you truths, lies, grace, intolerance, hope, and hopelessness. It's what you do with it, how you process it, act upon it, that matters in the end. At the end.

M: So why the lies, intolerance, hopelessness? Is it your test of me? Is it to awaken my innate common sense? Our innate common sense?

L: I'm the tester. I test your soul's frequency and development. Your fortitude vs. your weakness. Your grace vs. intolerance. Ego vs. humbleness. Greed vs. charity. Nice vs. kind.

M: Nice vs. kind?

L: Being nice does not always mean you're kind of soul. You can be nice to get what you want or need until being nice is no longer useful. Nice is not always genuine but is used as a tool of manipulation. Being kind is more genuine and soul-fulfilling. Kind is more in line with the Golden Rule, do unto others as you would have them do unto you.

M: So, being kind fits into "The meek shall inherit the earth," then?

L: Yes, but I guess you define the word "meek" based on conventional wisdom, conflating meek with weak.

M: Yes, I think of someone who is meek as submissive, gentle, malleable, and acquiescent, none of which garners confidence.

L: What is the opposite of meek?

M: I guess it would be aggressive, egotistical, pretentious, and stubborn.

L: Which one is more soul-strengthening?

M: Neither, in my opinion.

L: It's the lens you view the world through. Other words are associated with meek, like reserved, humble, unpretentious, self-disciplined, and self-effacing, and nothing in these traits are weak. Context is everything. Knowing you can defend yourself, be dangerous, if need be, but having the self-discipline, grace, and humbleness to not exercise those abilities unless absolutely necessary is not weak. Using violence when you could solve an issue by other means is weak.

M: Context *is* everything. In fact, I lose respect for individuals who purposely take things out of context to fit a particular narrative.

L: What about conjecture? Your news media is full of conjecture, and conjecture can lead to chaos, death, and destruction. It's your lack of patience and lack of impulse control that gives evil a firm footing. An unwillingness to wait for the facts allows people to manipulate with hyperbolic conjecture or diminish facts to create power through influence. Then, of course, there are promises and/or statements that are misleading for power and control. You witness it all around you.

M: So, like saying the last presidential election was stolen, and our current president is illegitimate?

L: Maybe it was stolen, and maybe it wasn't, but the lack of impulse control and patience has set in motion a chain of events that have damaged many souls' harmonic frequency. Evil wins; hell, I win as well because the fewer people feel a connection with one another, the easier it is to discount them as an essential part of society, therefore making them unnecessary and expendable. Are you following this line of reason?

M: Let me try to walk through it, high level. Hillary Clinton lost to Donald Trump and said Trump stole the election with Russian help and Trump knows he is an illegitimate president, which set off an unprecedented chain of events that have spiraled the United States into a chaotic political tailspin. This has hurt the American people and enriched the media to this day. Trump, for his part, ran on an antiestablishment, "drain the swamp" campaign, promising, threatening, and bullying his way to the presidency. He said the current governmental landscape was corrupt, and people needed to be held accountable. Lacking diplomacy with Democrats, many in his party and the mainstream media felt if he had any chance to make changes, he needed to hold the House and Senate, which the Republicans could not do. In retaliation to Trump's threats, the Democratic Party tried to impeach the president several times, drastically reducing his ability to get everything done he and his party wanted to accomplish. Of course, since all the impeachment attempts to remove him from office failed, one could believe the Democratic Party "might" resort to election tampering to achieve what the impeachment circus could not.

President Biden wins an election, which, of course, Trump says was stolen. Now, mainstream media and the new Biden administration call Trump's stolen election accusations the "Big Lie," and people who are election deniers are essentially labeled as domestic terrorists. Both sides despise each other, and given the lies, deception, ugliness, and corruption, both sides seem to embrace willingly and shamelessly to hurt each other, I don't see any hope unless both parties can drain their own swamps and put up decent, commonsense candidates. Shame on the populous for electing these awful, corrupt, hateful, deceptive, and low-vibrational human beings.

L: See how easy it is to lose oneself in righteous indignation, virtue singling, and judgment? Where is your grace?

M: I'm voicing my disappointment, but yes, I could have been more tactful in my rhetoric.

L: It's a common enough trait to be judgmental, as we discussed. It's being judgmental without discipline that is so destructive.

M: Explain if you would.

L: How about just three to start: weapons of mass destruction, COVID-19, and climate change. All these events were or are world-changing, and all have roots in manufactured and hyperbolic conjecture and media support and are incredibly destructive to the poor while enriching the wealthy and powerful. Furthermore, these three events were all exacerbated by using tremendous fear tactics to manipulate the world's majority into pouring trillions of dollars and destroying millions of lives based on manufactured intelligence, doubt, and corrupt scientists. Now, all three of these events have a common theme, fear, and each has its own benefactors . . . the world's military industrial complex, the pharmaceutical industry, and the green energy movement.

M: So, what are you suggesting? Each of these events was manufactured to create chaos for evil's gain?

L: Climate change is real, COVID is real, and weapons of mass destruction are real. The question people should be asking is . . . Are the responses appropriate to these events? Who are the winners, and who are the losers? Typically, the poor and middle class suffer the brunt of the diabolical decisions of the powerful and influential. And where do the powerful and influential get their bad ideas from, and who do you suppose is suppressing or even incentivizing the bypassing of common sense?

M: I'm sure you're going to blame it on evil. But I will say it's you and your followers who whisper and entice bad ideas and bad behaviors.

L: We do. But what does it say about those individuals who are so easily manipulated and taken off the path? Those who shut themselves off from positive energy and influence, which is readily available if one is open to it.

M: Angels?

L: Angels and demons, light and dark, good and evil. Would it surprise you to know that all of it is just a way to describe different energy frequencies that influence your soul's vibrational balance? It's positive and negative energy looking to find a home. But it can only find a home where it is accepted. We discussed this before.

M: No. I was curious about other dimensional influences like guardian angels or demonic possession. Are they a real thing?

L: Complicated, but let's repeat that each human is susceptible to high and low frequencies that influence their thoughts and actions. Demonic energy and angelic energy if it makes it easier to believe. Remember, you are energy. Your energy vibrates at a specific frequency, and it's that frequency that attracts other like frequencies. Demonic energy, or entities, constantly try to lower vibrational energy, while, in contrast, angelic energy tries to raise the harmonic frequency. Now, some attacks are more dangerous to your harmonic balance than others. Same with healing or raising of the harmonic frequency.

M: What are miracles?

L: Some say it's a miracle you haven't destroyed yourselves and the planet.

M: I can't argue that, but seriously, what are miracles?

L: Miracles are simply outcomes your small minds can't comprehend. You are seeds of the source with incredible untapped potential held back by ignorance, stupidity, lack of awareness, and lack of curiosity. But most of all, you're held back by entities like me, who influence the weak of mind and soul.

M: You're like a repeating loop—ignorance, stupidity, lack of curiosity, etc., etc. Okay, so let's get off this subject and go back to discussing evil. How do you know when an individual, group, or egregore is genuinely evil in intent and not just ignorant, stupid, etc.? Is there some way to figure it out?

L: Ha. There is no sure way! A wolf in sheep's clothing. True evil is rarely easily detectable. You say I'm evil. Yet, I say I'm doing God's work or the universe a favor. I test souls, and the weak, corrupt, and dark of spirit are exposed. You say that I am the reason people have weak, corrupt, and dark, or, let's say, low-vibrational souls. I say I just expose those that are prone to it. Evil is often in the eye of the beholder.

M: I know there is evil out there, and, of course, I want to expose it. I want to see it, and I want people to see it, and I want them to reject it. But unfortunately, it's difficult to know who the evil players and the unwitting supporters are. There is so much mind manipulation and propaganda that seemly quite sane people will take positions that make no common sense. Some we have covered during this conversation.

L: What are evil acts?

M: As we discussed, to hurt, destroy, and/or deceive for power, money, pleasure, and/or influence.

L: And that's it boiled down. Evil is a con game, and humanity is the victim. You think you can win but can't if you play its game and by its rules. And no matter how much your society, or the world, for that matter, wants to deny its tangible existence or that there is accountability, it makes no difference in the end. It is what it is, and humanity can't wish it away. So it's the burden of free will and the accountability that comes with it. I could continue to share more of my insights, but our time together must end for now. I've got other things to do, places to be, and people to tempt.

M: Well, you have certainly given me a lot to work through, but I will close with this. Humanity is better than you portray, and I think you know it. There is a lot of good in this world, and we have the potential to be everything we were created to be. We just need to shed the shackles you and evil have placed on us. So, for your time, your insights, true or, and I have no doubt of this, deceitful, I still thank you. Knowledge is a powerful tool for people willing to explore, challenge, evolve, and change.

L: Only time will tell.

Epilogue

First, thank you for sticking with me on this ride. For me, this project was a roller coaster of emotions, daunting, or maybe not as much daunting as it was a restlessness to find all the answers and yet, being resigned to the inevitability that I will never reach my goal of total enlightenment in this lifetime. Coming through this project, I can say, for me, the science is certainly not settled, and I'm not so sure how I feel about that. On the other hand, I can understand the desire to live one's life with absolute certainty. Not to question, explore, or be exposed to opposing points of view. I can see how simple life can be to unquestionably believe what you have been told without the need to exercise reason, common sense, or free will. And the freedom that comes with absolutely knowing you're right, and we know humans have an almost insatiable need to be correct. Maybe it's not so much about being right or wrong as it is about winning, and winning can come in all manner of shapes and sizes. But winning does not mean right. You can win an argument by shouting down or intimidating your opponent. You can win an election and not be truthful in your convictions. You can win a game by cheating. And, of course, I'm concerned about who is winning the battle for humanity's souls. One undeniable fact is the choices we make are ours. They can certainly be manipulated or even coerced, but they are ours. We own them, and only time will tell what impact they have on our souls.

I guess it's normal to worry if I'm on the right path or doing enough to stay on the right path. Then again, maybe it is not "normal" to have those concerns, which is such a sad and unfortunate state of our world. We are the architects of our soul, and we decide who we allow to influence our path through this life . . . who guides us, influences us, and molds us. And it is we who give licenses to trusted sources for that guidance. Parents, friends, teachers, professors, religion, politicians, social media, news media, work colleagues, and egregores? Is it all of them, some of them, or none? And where do all these outside influencers stack up regarding credible guidance? Who has your best interest in mind? And are you equipped to recognize the difference? And by "equipped," I mean, do you have the will and intellectual curiosity to find out, or are you just willing to go along to get along?

I can go on and on, but I will leave you with my final thoughts. Yes, I have messed up in the past. I've done things I should not have done, said things I should not have said, and thought things I should not have thought. Realistically, that will continue to be the case. However, if I do less of those things and do more things I should do, say things I should say, and think thoughts that should be thought, then I am headed in the right direction, and only time will tell if I've done enough. So, let's be willing to forgive ourselves for our past indiscretions by giving ourselves a little grace. If we can come to forgive ourselves first, we can begin to change the things we want to change. Everything we have done in the past, every choice, is behind us. There are few, if any of us, that have not stepped off the path that leads to our soul's harmonic balance, and that is okay. Recognition that there is a path and a willingness to learn how to walk it, is in my humble opinion, the most powerful thing we can ask of ourselves.

Be decent to yourself and others,

Best regards,

D. A. Dorward

www.ingramcontent.com/pod-product-compliance
Lightning Source LLC
Chambersburg PA
CBHW032131090426
42743CB00007B/559